The Fami

To John
at 70
with love

Marjorie.

The Family Budget

A remarkable collection of letters written by seven
Elmhirst brothers and their sister during the
First World War.

Edited with an Introduction, Epilogue and Biographies

by

Paul B. Elmhirst

THE ELMYRSTE PRESS

© Paul B. Elmhirst 2011

Published by The Elmyrste Press

ISBN 978-0-9568543-0-8

All rights reserved. Reproduction of this book by photocopying or electronic means for non-commercial purposes is permitted. Otherwise, no part of this book may be reproduced, adapted, stored in a retrieval system or transmitted by any means, electronic, mechanical, photocopying, or otherwise without the prior written permission of the author.

Cover design by Paul Elmhirst

Prepared and printed by:

York Publishing Services Ltd
64 Hallfield Road
Layerthorpe
York YO31 7ZQ

Tel: 01904 431213

Website: www.yps-publishing.co.uk

DEDICATED

To the memory of

WILLIAM ELMHIRST 1892 – 1916

and

ERNEST CHRISTOPHER ELMHIRST 1894 – 1915

ACKNOWLEDGEMENTS

Firstly, I must thank my wife Philippa for her advice and comments, but particularly for collecting the photographs, the cuttings, the extracts and the scratchy drawings on old letters and converting them into a manageable digital form. It was not a simple process, but without those images and her ability to rescue me when my computer misbehaved this book would still be a draft in a desk drawer.

Secondly, I must thank those members of the family who provided additional biographical material and missing information: Anne Fisher for notes on her mother Irene Rachel, Eloise Sharman for photos of her father Richard, Judy Webber for accounts (and several photos) of her father Vic, Jane Mackie for stories about her father Tommy (and for her energetic encouragement) and particularly Liz Haggard, (Richard's stepdaughter-in-law), for it was my rediscovery of her 25-year-old typed up copies of numerous FB letters which inspired me to track down the remaining letters and, ultimately, to bring them all together in this book.

Finally, I thank the Totnes Image Bank for Nicholas Horne's photo of Pom and Leonard in jovial mood at Dartington and the Devon Record Office for sending me two important letters written by Leonard after the deaths of his two brothers. I am indebted to Heather McIntyre and Yvonne Widger of the Dartington Hall Archive for their assistance and for providing several family photographs, including the evocative cover photograph. I am grateful to the staff of Sheffield City Archive who put themselves about to bring me the numerous boxes which held most of the missing letters and I thank Barnsley Archives for putting me in touch with Brian Elliot who provided me with the photograph of Irene Rachel at the opening of Barnsley Town Hall in 1933.

CONTENTS

Introduction	1
The letters:	
1914	7
1915	39
1916	106
1917	135
1918	164
1919	191
Epilogue	213
Biographies:	
William	215
Leonard	219
Christopher	223
Tommy	226
Victor	230
Richard	233
Alfred (Pom)	237
Irene Rachel	243
Map of Barnsley and district	247
Bibliography	248
Elmhirst Family Tree	249

ABOUT THE EDITOR/WRITER

Paul Elmhirst, who lives near York, is a retired solicitor. He has been married to Philippa for 40 years and they have two sons and four grandchildren. He is the second son of Alfred Octavius (Pom) and Gwen.

He was educated at Ward Green Primary School in Worsbrough, at Dartington Hall School and at Keele University, where he read Biology and Philosophy. He has also written "The Which? Guide to Wills and Probate".

In addition to tracking down these letters he has enjoyed writing the biographical "Brief Lives" of his father, his aunt and the uncles whom he knew well as that has enabled him to incorporate a number of interesting and amusing family stories that might otherwise be forgotten.

INTRODUCTION

My grandfather, William Heaton Elmhirst, was born at Gainsborough in 1856, the year in which the Crimean War ended. He died in 1948 at "Elmhirst" on the outskirts of Barnsley at the age of 92, having lived through two world wars. I remember him as a frail old man with a white beard. He had eight sons followed by one daughter and, although he was a curate in the early years of his marriage, he seems to have spent much more time shooting and fishing than preaching. My grandmother, Mary Elmhirst, was a devout woman who must have been much tougher than she looked. To some of her less respectful relatives she was known as "The Hardy Annual".

Dad was the eighth son (hence Octavius, although "Pom" became his name within the family and to intimates). Their last child and only daughter was Irene Rachel. My uncles were William, born 1892, Leonard Knight, born 1893, Ernest Christopher, born 1894, Thomas Walker, born 1895, Edward, born 1897 (but died a few months later), James Victor, born 1898, and Richard, born 1900. My father, Alfred Octavius, born 1901, and my aunt, Irene Rachel, born 1902, brought up the rear.

Laxton Church with Christie, Tommy, Willie and Leonard in the foreground. Possibly 1898.

Papa and Mama at Elmhirst with spaniel in 1905.

My grandfather started married life in the Vicarage at Laxton, near Howden in the East Riding of Yorkshire, where all nine children were born. In 1899, after the death of his father, he inherited the family estate and in 1903 they all moved to Pindar Oaks in Barnsley. On the death of his mother in 1916, they moved up the road into the family home at Elmhirst in Worsbrough.

As a child I heard Dad speak of "The Family Budget", but in those days I had no idea what it was. Later on I discovered that it was not my grandfather's attempt to balance available cash against the cost of keeping a wife and eight children, but a rather obscure definition, meaning a bag or sack and its contents. The Family Budget was conceived in 1914 by Uncle Leonard as a way to keep brothers and sister in touch with one another during the war without each having to write seven letters at a time.

Papa with pony and trap arriving at Elmhirst with Mama in the front entrance. About 1917.

The principles were set out by Leonard in October 1914.

"Rules of game and how played:

<u>Reason.</u> I have no time to write to everyone perpetually, neither have most of us, therefore I put up for approval this scheme.

1. Enclosed is a letter from me, this goes to Christie, he sends it on with one written with his own paw to one of the rest so that Willie, Leonard, Christie, Tommy, Vic, Richie, Alf and Irene each get it in turn.
2. I suggest that the letter whilst in England goes to each of us in turn and Irene last, then she writes hers, puts it in and sends it off to Tommy. Daddy and Mother can then see the whole lot before they go.
3. Unfortunately, we have to wait until it comes back, which under present conditions might be never, but no matter. Tommy forwards it back to me. I take out my scrawl, put a new one in and send on to Christie, but it must go on in the same order that it went round first, each taking out his old one and putting in a new one. Now you all understand and say no if you don't approve. Well, here goes."

These rules contained in Leonard's letter set up the "FB", as it was called. Although the brothers and their sister were never very diligent correspondents and although none had any outstanding literary gifts, the FB continued to circulate for the next five momentous years during which time the brothers played their parts in the First World War or Great War (which was always referred to by Dad as the "Kaiser War").

Willie became a captain in the 8th Btn East Yorks Regiment and was posted to France, only to be killed on the Somme. Leonard, passed as unfit for military service, was sent to India and Mesopotamia as a representative of the YMCA where he organised relief for citizens and soldiers alike. Later, in 1918, on his return to England, he enlisted and was placed in the Officers Cadet Battalion of the 2nd Artists' Rifles for a brief period. Christie, as a second lieutenant in the 8th Duke of

Wellington's, was despatched to Gallipoli where he died in action at Suvla Bay. Tommy, who always intended to make his career in the Navy, spent the early years of the war as a mid-shipman on board the battleship H.M.S. Indomitable. Later on, in the RNAS[1], he hunted U-boats in an R-100 airship. Vic, after leaving Marlborough, emerged from Sandhurst as a second lieutenant and was posted to Mesopotamia with the York and Lancasters where one of his missions was to take a group of men by camel into the area between Tehran and Basra, "to see what the damned Bolsheviks were up to". When Richie left Rugby at the end of the war, he was commissioned into the Coldstream Guards. Dad (Pom) spent the whole war at Winchester College, while Rachel completed her schooling at The Manor House, Brackley. Both of them tried to learn their lessons and both, occasionally, excelled at shooting, cricket and rat catching.

Pom (as a toff) at Winchester sporting a top hat.

These Family Budget letters, most of which had somehow survived in various boxes and packets, paint a fascinating picture of the life of one family set against the storm-laden backdrop of the Great War. There is an endearing warmth between the brothers and their sister, as well as occasional and poignant references to the risk of death. Most of all, these letters confound our assumptions: the Elmhirsts could be described as Landed Gentry, but they lived among the pits of Barnsley; their parents were Victorian, but were not always stern; they all attended public schools, yet none could be called a "toff" (except perhaps the youthful Pom when photographed in his top hat). And, like every up and coming generation, they took the new technology in their stride.

---

1   Royal Naval Air Service.

Even after the deaths of brothers Christie and Willie, the FB continued to circulate among the survivors. What did they all make of it? Perhaps the feelings were best expressed by Dad when I asked him, in the early 1960s at the time of the war in Vietnam, what he and his friends at Winchester thought about the Great War. He said: "We all accepted the war with a fatalism that is now hard to understand. We joined the school OTC[2] with enthusiasm. We knew we would enlist on leaving school, become second lieutenants and we knew that most of us would be dead within a year. It was an obligation. We saw it as our duty." He went on to describe how name after name of those boys who had left Winchester in one year would be inscribed on the roll of honour in the school hall a year later. Brother Richie, in a letter dated 21st June 1915, refers to a memorial service at Rugby for 52 old boys who had been killed in the previous two months.

Here are those letters. I have resisted the temptation to edit them (apart from creating some paragraphs and adding a considerable number of full stops) as I think that the detail of the unedited letters gives a better insight into the characters of the correspondents and their relationships with one another. I have added two letters which are not part of the FB. One was written by Pom to Christie in July 1915 and the other was written by Christie to Auntie Min in July 1915, only a week or so before he was killed. The FB letters which followed the deaths of Christie and Willie make no reference to those tragedies: what could they say? It was probably too painful. But whatever the reason for the silence, there can be no doubt that all the survivors of this close knit family deeply lamented the loss of their two brothers.

That is clear from Leonard's letter to his mother, sent from Ahmednagar on the 8th October 1915 following news of Christie's death. In it he expresses his deeply held Christian beliefs and outlines to his mother, a devout Christian herself, his views on death, faith and the resurrection. He wrote: "But here there is nothing for which I can offer more humble and hearty thanks than for Christie's life and death. I can only think of Christie's death as a happy end to a happy life and now I feel nearer

---

2   Officer Training Corps.

than ever. And not only that, but I believe we understand each other better than before."

By the time Leonard wrote from Basra to his father on the 6th January 1917 following news of Willie's death, however, his attitude had changed completely. The comfort of faith is missing. He wrote: "And so Willie is gone. I cannot get myself to believe it and I am the eldest son. The letters of appreciation only make me feel more bitter about what, in many ways, seems the uneccessary wastage of war." He continues: "In the last few months my whole outlook on life has changed. It is too long to explain, but the effect of it is that, for the time being, I do not see the way open to taking Holy Orders and I could not honestly put my name to most of the things the Church demands." Perhaps he spoke for the others when he said: "What useless things words are at a time like this. So far I've been absolutely unable to express anything that I feel."

I have written the introduction, the epilogue and the biographies in a personal way because that seemed to me to be the best way to present these intimate communications. The biographies are not intended to give a complete picture, but I have attempted to catch the character of each person with numerous family anecdotes. I am sure I have missed a lot of important incidents and I may well have misrepresented some members of the family in my effort to make the biographies readable. If I have, I apologise.

I have also added footnotes to all those letters where further explanation or background is needed.

From Leonard. Trinity College, Cambridge.
18th October 1914.

Dear Christie, We discussed this scheme if you remember and I've gone and given it a kick off but I ought not to start like that. You must try and think of a good start, I can't.

Dear Beasts (& Beastess),

I hope this will find you as it leaves me at present in the best of health and spirits except that there is so much work to be done and little time to do it. In a weeks time we expect to have 200 students from Tourain up in Cambridge and they will have to be looked after. Meanwhile, instead of 600 men up there are about 250, of whom 128 are freshers, most of whom know no one and have to be let down gently. It is an awkward process; you go in and say, "Is it Mr So and So?" Mr S & S says, "Yes it is". "Well", you say, "Mr Somebody else asked me to call on you". "Oh, very good of him to be sure" says he. Then silence. "Oh have a cigarette", says he. "Well I can only stay a minute", says I, "but come into a meal sometime". This way out of the difficulty sometimes refuses to act because he says nothing when you get him there, but so far I have taken the cigarette and stopped for 30mins instead of one.

I have met lately 2 Americans, very fresh from America, who are doing the University life. One is trying to get into the Corps and has dropped onto his feet here very quickly, the other is *very* American. His accent will give him away to any recruiting officer.

So far I have spent my time attending some dozen meetings, committee and otherwise, sending out some 200 invitations to be addressed and printed. The answers to them and the different styles in which they are done almost repay in interest what has been lost in time. Games have practically been washed out, O.T.C holds the field, but it is little or no use in my joining. They have lectures five nights a week, drill 3 hours for 4 afternoons per week and one night operations, which means that they do no work and will all have commissions by Xmas. Next term there will be about two men left.

I have been staying in London, as you may know, for three weeks, have seen Christie 3 times looking very <u>braw</u> and rolling in wealth, cousin Maud also and, for two nights, the family took possession of her mistresse's house.

Congratulations to Vic on getting his shave, this letter is not to prevent him, or anyone else writing to me because I shan't see the budget until it has been to Tommy. One of our courts has been a military hospital and various interesting men were in it. One man whilst coming round after an anaesthetic went through the whole of the action again, shouting, "Buck your men up Mr Verrall" and then, "Come on Yorkshire", at the top of his voice.

Well now goodbye.

Your affectionate brother L.K.Elmhirst.

From Christie. 3 Company
4th P.S. BATT. ROYAL FUSILIERS
ASHSTEAD
SURREY
19th Oct 1914

Dear Willie etc. down to Irene,

Your first business is to read the rules of the game, then Leonard's letter then mine & so on. I expect I shall be in France by the time my turn for the budget comes back to me. Rumours are already abroad that we are going into Barracks in the South of France in a few weeks' time, but I do not think it is very likely.

Well, I am leading a strenuous life here & the work is now beginning to get interesting as we are practising attacking, judging distances, skirmishing, etc. which are a great improvement on forming fours, platoon & Company drill; we have a Battalion parade nearly every day & route march about once a week. We started life in the army with 7 hours a day solid work, then came down to 5½ when the Adjutant arrived & are now gradually getting back to 7 hours again. On Oct. 12, 13 & 14 we went to help to make our huts at Woodcote Park; my friend, His Majesty the King[1] came and watched me sawing a plank in two, he seemed quite interested; that was on the Monday. If you see any photos of hut building look out for me on the top of the roof nailing the roofing boards on; the other principal jobs were putting the floors down & carting wood about.

At present our pay has amounted to £2 but it soon goes when you meet a fellow in Town now and again who always has the same tale to tell, 'I'm stony' for example Leonard, I don't know how he exists. I got my bicycle today. It will be awfully useful as Ashstead village is about a mile away. My hostess keeps & looks after us very well, her husband is a double blue of Hertford Coll, Oxford & plays cricket for Essex, name, C.D. McIver. I hope Willie's got his commission & that Vic had a decent birthday & will not leave this batch of letters in his writing case for a week or so; I

---

1 George V.

also hope Richard is enjoying life generally & Alfie's 'sugarstick' fracture[2] (something like that) is better & lastly that all the livestock at Pindar Oaks is surviving under the tender care of Irene. My bedtime here is about 9.30 & so I must stop. Goody-bye all

From your affectionate brother

E. Chris. Elmhirst (Pte)

---

2 There are various facetious references to Pom's "greenstick" fracture.

From Willie. 10, Burton Stone Lane
York
Sunday. Oct. 25. 1914

Dear Sirs & Madam

Christie's of Oct. 19th to hand. I am afraid it has reposed in my pocket for four days, but I am leading a strenuous life at present & don't feel inclined for much letter writing in an evening. I work from 10 to 1 & 2 to 6 or 6.30 or 7 every day so sometimes don't get back for my dinner till 7.15. I work at a big table (all to myself) with a telephone & a typewriter by my side in a picture gallery 100 feet long. All the pictures have been taken down some time ago & we have put Recruiting Posters & notices of Recruiting meetings up instead, just to encourage recruits when they come in. I haven't got my commission yet though I expected to hear this last week.

I lunched with Uncle Charlie today & had two of Mrs. Wade's mince pies. The best I ever tasted. She's noted for them. Don was quite fit and finished off the hare bones when Uncle Charlie & I had done with them. If I go out to the Front, a friend of mine has offered to lend me a revolver. He's an Ulsterman & has got several & some rifles as well, which were waiting to go to Ulster before the War began.

Charles. E. Elmhirst, solicitor in York and brother of W.H. Elmhirst. He was also the Hon Secretary of the Yorkshire Philosophical Society. 1931.

We had a General came into the Recruiting Office a few days ago & I had to explain the whole process of enlisting a man & then he wanted to know how many clerks we should want if we had to deal with three or four hundred men a day instead of thirty.

It looks rather as if there would soon be some sort of conscription. We have got about 300 refugees in York now & I suppose about 1500 aliens in a big enclosure. There is a tremendous big hall at the Exhibition Buildings, where I work, which will hold about 2000 people. On Friday night they were expecting 1000 German soldiers to come & be put there but they didn't arrive & only 9 aliens turned up. The prisoners will probably come in this week. We had 1000 aliens there three weeks ago, all sorts, waiters & barbers & well to do people, & then we had three hundred Territorials there in a smaller hall.

There are about 10,000 Territorial troops coming into York this week. They will nearly all be billeted in private houses & big buildings. Would any one like the Lord Mayor's signature & coat of arms or the signatures of Mr. Butcher K.C., M.P. for York? I don't know if anyone collects them now. Praps Pom knows someone who would like them.

I have made Canon Watson's acquaintance. I think most of the family have heard him preach. He told me he was preaching four sermons a Sunday just now. I've heard him twice at the Minister lately. I got over to Arkendale for a Sunday a fortnight ago. I only took a toothbrush with me in case they didn't ask me to stop. However they did & Uncle Harry[1] provided me with some beautiful blue pyjamas & a razor etc.

I went home last Sunday & we had 12 in our pew at Worsbro[2] as it was Harvest Festival.

P.S. for Pom. I haven't told Mr. Clarke yet. Thank you for your letter. I hope the arm is better.

P.S. Monday 8.30. Just heard from Daddy that I have got my commission, but I haven't had anything official myself yet.

Much love to you all from your loving brother,

William Elmhirst

---

1 Harry Knight, his mother's brother.
2 The family enjoyed a box pew at the back of St Mary's Church, Worsbrough. Beneath it is a vault in which members of the family were interred until 1851 when a law was passed forbidding burial within a church.

From Vic. Preshute House
Marlborough
Oct 1914.

Dear All

I hope you are feeling quite fit including Alfie whose arm is nearly all right now I should think. I hope that will do for a start. It's different from the others anyhow. I saw a photo of Christie sitting on his little wooden hut with a hammer in his hand. The photo was in the Sporting and Dramatic News, a paper which we get for some unknown reason as no one really wants it.

We see simply heaps of motor transports going past here. I saw more than 100 going past this afternoon. Old motorbuses painted grey with about 3 soldiers to each one. They sleep inside at night. I think we saw a few blankets inside. We were coming from footer at the time and we stopped and cheered each one. The soldiers looked very decent and are all very jovial.

I am playing full-back at rugger on Lower, and if the back on Upper got ill I might have a chance of playing in his place which would be very fine. We have only had three games so far because of the ground and on Lower we have won two with about 50 and 30 nil and lost the other about 50 to nil against us. It is quite good fun, though today a boy went and put his wrist out. Not a very pleasant sight or feeling. Perhaps Alfie will tell us what it is like.

I had a very good birthday, a nice lot of food and cash, and lots of letters and post cards. Much too many for answering in fact. I got a cake from Mrs Taylor, a very nice one.

A little time ago we had a lot of Belgian Refugees down here. We gave them a good tea and lots of cheering, they really stood it quite well! And I have heard that a lot of Germans are going to be shut up on the Downs somewhere about 2 miles from us. There are a lovely lot of Spanish Chestnut Trees in the forest and the Sunday before last, Oct 18th, I got such a lot that I was nearly ill from eating them!! and I had to give a lot away. There are quite a lot of deer about but they are or were dangerous as it is the mating season so you do not go looking for them. I have to go to prep now so I shall finish off later.

There is a scandal going about here that instead of exams in the last week of term we are going to have drill and cap work. I hope it is true, but I do not expect it is. We have an extra afternoons drill now and we have already had 3 minor field days from about 2 – 7 o'clock. Jolly good fun specially when it gets dark. Hurrah for Willie's commission!!!! I hope he gets into some decent regiment that he will like.

P.S. I hope this is considered to be enough. P.S. I have been beaten once but owing to a nice <u>hanky</u> folded <u>twice</u> it did not hurt very much. The <u>Man</u> was very funny, he said I was a disgraceful boy for giving him so much exercise.

Much love to all from your loving brother   Vic Elmhirst

From Richie   4 Horton Crescent, Rugby
29th Oct 1914.

Dear Family,

I think this budget a very good thing. I am getting on very well. I have only been beaten once.

We have been stopped sugar in our porridge and tea; it is sweetened before it comes in. I am fagging for the sixth room this week, it's an awful fag. We have won both house matches we have played. The first we won 37-nil, the second was most exciting, against the schoolhouse, who are cock-house. We beat them 9 to 3. Our captain and theirs both had to stop once, they had both got good hacks. We have a very good chance for cock-house.

I put in a 1/- for a raffle for a chap who had gone to Sandhurst and got a 1st choice and an 8th choice. For 1st I got a pair of pictures for which I have been offered 6/-. So glad to hear that Willie has got a commission. We have got about 150 Belgians in Rugby. There was a debate on Saturday as to whether we should put four of them in the pavilion.

Auntie Min came a little time ago. She asked me out to tea with Peter[1] at the school shop, but there was not a half that day, so I got 2/- and some pears. I hope she comes again this term. I have spent nearly 10/- on the study this term, it looks ripping now. Hawker[2] (cousin C) comes round the studies once a week and picks out the untidy ones, to whom he says he will give 200 lines. The other day a chap put a book over the door of the form room for the maths master, who is very slack, but the chap got 500 lines and no alternative!! My form master nick-named "Spittler mi" has gone as a Tommy to somewhere so we have got a new form master. He is much nicer.

---

1   Peter, son of Charles Edward Hawkesworth (Hawker) and cousin Nan.
2   Hawker was Richard's housemaster at Rugby. He was married to Nan, a daughter of Auntie Min.

On Fridays we have debates sometimes, or he asks who will give a lecture and we have had some very good ones. One week I was 4th in my form and I was moved up into another maths set this term and was 7th for the half-term. I cannot get any higher till I get into another form. There is not much news here, but "every little helps for the family budget"!!

Much love to you all from your loving brother,

Richard Elmhirst.

From Alfred. Stancliffe Hall, Matlock.
30th October 1914.

Dear Messes and Mad arm.

I hope you are all alive and kicking. I am kicking, but not alive. Oh bosh it!! That's wrong, tother way round!! My arm is getting on all right. It was what you call a "greenstick fracture" which is supposed to be worse than breaking it, so I was told.

Please will you (Irene) put the date on the instruction card on the day that you send the whole Budget off to Tommy who it is your business to send it to. Mind you write 4 pages or over. You can recognise Christie on that P.P.C. quite easily can't you? I haven't started games yet, but I expect I shall have done by the time that this comes back. I am doing quite well here. I haven't had a swishing yet, but I don't think I can do the term without it though!!!

There is a craze for knitting here also, so I thought that I would start. I am writing this in the big schoolroom at a master's desk, awful swank isn't it!!!! I expect you will think this is the real Budget when it arrives. Don't you think Leonard is fearfully brainy to invent it (I suppose it was he). We have played two matches this term and 3 tomorrow. We have won 1 and lost 1. 4-0 and 0-4. We play Shardlow Hall tomorrow.

Leonard is becoming quite a man isn't he?!! Isn't Vic a pig over-eating himself with chestnuts. It was unlucky for Richie, not being a half hol on which Aunty Min invited him out to tea. It is amusing to see all the war papers etc arriving by the post. Nearly everybody gets one; Great War, War Illustrated, Illustrated War News, Daily Sketch etc and about half a dozen more.

We are having special Intercession Services now twice a week. To Leonard: It was St Anselms that we beat 4-0. I haven't had an 'Impot' yet from Mr Wheen, Woodhill, Conway, Clarke, only a history paper from Mr Owen and some Caesar because a chap made the whole class stay in a half hol, so I am industrious aren't I. It's Friday night to-night and we do dancing. I'm not allowed to do so, now I must continue afterwards as the bell has gone for school. I might as well finish now it's school time.

So much love to you all from your loving brother,

Alfred

From Irene Rachel.   Pindar Oaks
Barnsley
Guy Fawkes day,
Nov 5th 1914

Dear Comrade's,

I hope you are all getting on all right, I think the budget a very good idea. Aunt Em and Uncle Bert have been staying here for about a week looking after their new house. I went up there to day and had a look round, it will be nice when it is finished. Daddy has got a motor car now, Henry can drive quite well. There is "AA" on a little thing on the frunt that means "Automobile Association". I asked Henry what it ment and he told me that if a motor breaks down on a country road with AA on it and another motor comes by with AA on, it has to help the broken down one, even if it is in a very great hurry. So when I go out I hope that we sharn't meet a broken down one with AA on it.

My farmyard are doing very well, except in the ferret family where there has been a death. The white baby ferret died a few weeks ago (not because of me tho). He got rheumatics and the other two were rather rough with him. The bants are quite well, but [neither] Mrs nor the Miss Bantys have begun to lay yet which is very bad of them. Doctor is out in the field with Dartmoor and Pindar the foal is as big as Dartmoor now and very dirty and rough. They all come after me when I go to feed the hens. Daddy has sold Fireaway. A man in Barnsley bought her and then sold her to the Adjutant here and she lives at Mr Hewitts house with some others.

Kitson the gardener caught 18 rats in two days in the stable with traps and five in the wire trap. Daddy, Kitson and I and Conus[1] had some lovely fun with the ones in the wire trap, Kitson brought them in the trap onto the pan cake[2], and let out one at a time. Conus had them before they ran a yard, two of them he caught before they got quite out of the trap. There is a rat in the house and it got into the boot room &

---

1   Conus was the family terrier.
2   The pancake was the round patch of grass in front of Pindar Oaks.

Conus in 1915 – rat catcher and companion.

could not get out. We had the ferrets in, but they could not find it, then the next morning it nearly got out. It scratched under the boot room door a lot of wood and dust, there was quite a big heap, then Conus and I had a hunt. Conus tipped over a crate of sections nearly on himself and then I had to spend about ten minutes picking them up again, also he tipped over two bee crates. He spends half the day there. Yesterday when Clara came down in the morning to the kitchen it was looking at her through a big hole under the kitchen door, but she made a noise at it and then ran away. There are two big holes each side of the kitchen door about as big as this.

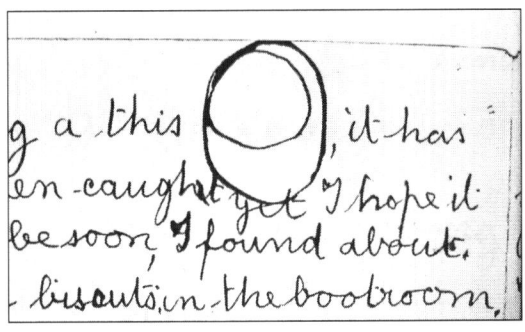

The rat hole referred to in Irene Rachel's letter of 5th November 1914.

It has not been caught yet but I hope it will be soon. I found about three biscuits in the bootroom. I have been making toffee. It was good and as hard as nuts and Conus liked it too. I have eaten heaps of it. To Tommy: Uncle Bert's new house is Mrs Gradwell's old one, Pindar Oaks Cottage, Aunty Em is going to call it 'The Cottage' because our letters will be always mixing with theirs. Where the licky bull dog used to live, she had a puppy some time ago.

I went to Art class this afternoon and I go to dancing class tomorrow morning. Granny and the aunts are all very well. I got some fire works to day to send off in the kitchen, it will be fun. To Tommy, we did like your letter about the Goeben[3] praps you will do for her yet, and it will be a good thing if you do, I hope you will keep off the mines.

Good bye all

From your loving sister Irene

---

3   The Goeben was a German warship.

From Tommy.
                                              At Sea.
                                              H.M.S. Indomitable
                                              2nd Battle Cruiser Squadron.
                                              22nd Nov 1914.

Dear "Sirs & Madam, beasts and beastess, Willie etc to Irene, All, Family, Messes and Mad arm, and Comrades."

Yesterday evening 21st Nov. a collier arrived at Tenedos (close to the Dardanelles) bringing with it the "Family Budget" besides a little coal, (5000 tons) a submarine and a few other things, so we shall be able to send mail tomorrow & I'm writing today Sunday so as to delay it as little as possible.

I think the family budget is a very good idea, but I benefit by it more than anyone else as you others will have to wait some time while it comes out here and gets back again. However, it has only taken 16 days to come and I expect not more than ten to go back. I suggest that instead of each one taking out his own old letter they are all taken out at home. They will make quite interesting reading later on.

Two hours after the arrival of the "F.B." we had orders to proceed on a 700 mile trip at full speed, so we are now rattling along burning about 40 tons of coal an hour. I am afraid I can not tell you our destination[1] or what we are going to do[2], but we are all very glad to be doing something as our blockade was getting very monotonous.

We have not been able to do very much to Turkey as there are a lot of English people still living in Turkey and if we do much more they will all get massacred so we are marking time a little. Our "demonstration bombardment" gave them a tremendous fright and made a great impression, which was what it was meant to do. Our ships were HMS Indomitable and HMS Indefatigable, (the old French ships hardly counted). During the ten minutes firing from the 12 guns (six guns from each fired) we put fifty 900 lb shells into the forts, destroying one

---

1 They were off to Port Said to convoy the first Indian Army contingent from Port Said to Marseilles.

2 Blockading the German Battle Cruiser "Goeben".

fort with six 11 inch guns and probably some more, a large magazine, a wireless station, and killed 500 men. Not bad for 10 minutes.

The British Consul, who was near at the time said if we had done a little more all the forts would have been evacuated and the Turkish officers were astounded at the accuracy of our fire. We landed our first shots right in the forts at 8 miles which was pretty good and we kept our range even though altering course and going at a good speed. We all wished we had been able to keep on at it a bit more. Their firing was bad besides being very slow.

My station is inside one of our 12" turrets, so I did not see much of the actual firing but I came on top directly we had finished and had the pleasure of hearing a large shell whistle over my head. We have had small excitements, such as picking up mines that have come out of the Dardanelles, but nothing very much since. The worst part of blockading as we have been doing is the fact that we get no chance of going ashore and consequently very little exercise besides which we get very poor food.

We are having a pretty strenuous time here, always steaming up and down except when we go and anchor in some quiet spot for coaling which is a pretty frequent and regular operation. However, we get pretty quick on it generally taking in about 1400 tons in six hours every week, sometimes oftener. We go to "night defence" stations during the dark hours which now means from about 4.30 PM until 6 AM. Some of the time you are actually looking out and the remainder you sleep at your station, either controlling a group of 4" guns or a group of searchlights. It is pretty cold work at present as there is always a wind when you are steaming and we are having a good deal of rain. We generally play deck hockey in the afternoons, it is quite a good game but rather dangerous.

I am afraid we have seen the last of the Goeben, which is a great pity. It would have been a real good fight if we had met. We are all very glad we have not had to fight the Austrians[3]. Their Naval Officers are a real good

---

3 Before 1919 "Austria" had several meanings. Here it must mean the Austrian part of the Austro-Hungarian Empire ruled by Franz Joseph until 1916. The population included Ukrainians, Poles, Czechs and Austrians.

sort and when we went to Pola and Trieste, their two Naval ports, in the early summer, they gave us the time of our lives and spared absolutely nothing in entertaining us. We continued the acquaintance in June when they came to Malta. They have only got a small but very efficient Navy, the French seem to find them a hard nut to crack. They have got their whole fleet up the Adriatic, but never seem to get anything done.

My congratulations to Willie on his commission and appointment to the East York's. They seem to have had more than their share of officers killed and wounded in the Expeditionary force. I hope he and C[4] will be able to see "Active Service" soon. It came as quite a shock to me when I heard of the motor at home [20 HP Austin Landaulette]. I did not know there were even thoughts of getting one. I hope I shall be home soon to enjoy it.

Well this must finish my contribution. I shall look forward to the "F.B." coming on its next circuit. Best of luck to Willie and Christie. I hope that Leonard will provide good refuge to the Cambridge Refugees, that Vic will not get beaten again, that Richard's family are doing well and that Pom will soon regain his health and strength?

Best of love to you all from your ever affectionate Brother,

Tommy

---

4 Christie.

From Leonard Elmhirst.   Trinity College, Cambridge.
                                          7th December 1914.

There, at last, I've got through the lot. And thank you all very much for playing the game, strictly to rule. Tommy's tops the whole thing up well. It's all splendid and most impressive.

Just a few remarks before I start off.

1. The 4 page idea is good, let's stick to it.

2. If we send it on quickly, it will get past Irene before we little ones get home and will be off to Tommy before Christmas.

3. Yes, as Tommy suggests, why not keep the old ones in until the letter arrives there and let them be collected. If they keep up to the present standard they will make very good reading later. Our parents, I know, have a strong and good objection to storing correspondence, but there are a few crannies in my little drawer upstairs which would hold them.

And now to start in earnest.

Dear (for crisp brevity Vic has it). I'm in no condition for serious thinking tonight so I shall leave it out.

I have had an exciting and busy time especially last Sat night when at 10 I was woken by terrific hammerings on the door which was locked, then on the window. I thought the Germans were upon me, so I lay low and said nuffink, but in the distance came cries of "fire". It gives you the creeps. I was up like greased lightning, into a dressing gown and out in the cold with two shakes of a duck's beak.

There sure enough lighting the already well moonlit heavens, were crackling flames and piles of smoke, coming from the roof of one of our courts. It was a good bonfire and really did very little damage, but it burnt out two of the top sets of rooms on the staircase and flooded the whole of the other six, also burning along inside the false roof. One man just underneath slept through it all until woken by peculiar sounds he leapt out into four inches of water. The fire-engine dashed up (the college apparatus being academic, failed at the critical moment).

Up went the firemen, the flames quickly vanished, but they had to un-roof a lot, sat astride of the roof. I watched them at work, warming my cold feet on the hot tiles. Then back to bed at 3.am.

This week I go down, up to London, to conduct a party of about 15 pleasant men down to a poor parish across the Thames[1] where they will see all the sights and find that life to some people is not always comfortable, but often merely a struggle to get enough food to exist on and, as for pleasure, well there is only the public house and that is just now generally shut. It makes me curl up almost to see it and, what is worse, we can do nothing.

Tomorrow evening I act chairman to a Society[2] in Trin formed this term which has now some 60 members including 10 dons, the two deans, four or five fellows and a lecturer or two. It will be our second general meeting, though we meet in little groups all through the term and discuss all kinds of things. You would like to hear perhaps my programme today.

Up at 7.25, dressed bathed and spruce by 7.30. Breakfast 8.0 at a café in the town with a Society which holds them every fortnight and has a man down to talk. Everyone knows everyone else and it is all very jolly, cream with the porridge too. Nine o'clock to ten, reading and correcting an essay to be read to my director of studies at 12.30. Ten o'clock, on with my gown and square and off to get my bicycle and cycle half a mile to a lecture on the Italian Renaissance and Machiavelli. Notes steadily for an hour, then at 11 to 12 notes to be taken on Modern History for another hour. Back to my den, where an officer [who] came up for the weekend, arrives to say goodbye. I settle down to read through essay again and in comes don to talk about two other dons who want to join my Society, I can't think why. One is a lecturer in Hebrew and an atheist, the other I don't know quite what. 12.00, round to director and spouting my essay

---

1 This was Trinity's mission in Camberwell, London.
2 This is probably the multi-denominational Student Christian Movement of which Leonard was a keen supporter.

to him but at 1.10 to lunch with a funny man who has very little to say for himself but we keep the ball rolling fairly well until 1.45. Then out to fix up something about our trip to London.

Back to rooms, where I find Salter[3]. Christie knows of him, Mother and Daddy have seen him, a don of Magdalene and probably coming to stay with me next vac. Whilst talking to him, I suddenly catch sight of a fat letter in my door, from Tommy. A thousand cheers, forget all about Salter, tear it open, the <u>family budget</u>. (A passing thought; what fun the censor must have had reading them all through) However it was 2.15 and I was due at the house of Dr. Raffaello Piccoli, who teaches me Italian at 2.15, so off I rushed. Having learned Italian for an hour and a half, back here to get tea ready. At 4.00 in comes Salter (aforesaid) and we discuss as to how Cambridge Dons want reforming. At 4.30 in comes (whom do you think ?) John (or is it Philip) J.J to a t. (joke). Salter went, but he having no work and I having heaps, stayed on far too long leaving me only time to read the budget and write this before going to guzzle at 7.45.

After that I hope for one hours work unless I am disturbed. At 9.15 I go out again to my director of studies to finish off my essay and tell me what to do in the vac, work. We shall probably talk on till 11.0 then we'll hop to bed, well earned do you think?

In comes a man with two subscriptions to be banked, noted, receipted and docked. Well, congratulations to Christie (I only wrote to him yesterday) on his commission. I think I should like to be one of his "Tommies". Pom, be quite well by the vac, ditto Richie. Hurrah for Vic and his football colours, he has sent me vivid descriptions for which thanks. Irene, I think your letter takes the biscuit, it's champion. Tommy, shoot straight and get this beastly butchery over and done with as quickly as you can. The photo is ripping, cannot anyone put in a photo of Christie doing Brer Rabbit on the roof of his house, any photos by the way will be welcome. Willie, do you have a nose protector I wonder when examining 400 feet after a 10 hours march?

Love to all from Leonard,

---

3   This will be Frank Salter, otherwise referred to as "The Psalter".

From Christie.   8th Duke of Wellington's
                                                                                              Belton Park
                                                                                              Grantham
                                                                                              Dec 9 1914.

Mes chers freres et soeur (is that right?)

On arriving back in the ante-room of the officer's mess I observed in my pigeon hole an eeeenormous letter, notably the 'F.B.'. It took me quite ½ an hour to read through all the letters which were most interesting & amusing & for which I thank you all.

Well, there have been many changes since the last time I put my letter in the 'F.B.' which was about 7 weeks ago, 'for now I am a Hossifer in the King's Armee' and when all's said & done it is better than being <u>a</u> Tommy (not Tommy). If anyone mentions my Regiment say it is the "Duke of Wellington's" and not the "West Riding". We hope to go out next January but as I am the junior Subaltern I shall most probably stay behind for a short while unless they cannot get along without me, which is quite possible. The strength of Officers in this Battalion will soon be 30, at present we are 28 (I am 28th). As some may know, I got gazetted on Nov 18 I think, appointed to the above about Nov 25 & joined here Nov 27 Friday. I am in the 8th (Service) Battln. Duke of Wellington's of the 34th Brigade of the 11th Division of Northern Command, we are all in huts. At present there are 16 Officers in this hut, which is divided up into 8 partitions.

Christie, Tommy and Willie showing off their uniforms while on leave in 1914 – plus Conus.

I have doubled up with a fellow called Jolley who is a Hertford (Oxford) man & quite lively (no don't make a pun); we purchase all our own stuff & get a Govt. grant of £7 – 10s – 0d for it. Most of my stuff folds up; I have a folding bed (like Leonard's), fold up bath, wash stand & basin, bucket, chair & table, & they all go into one kit bag which I have got; other things I have got are a Valise, a sleeping bag & a pr. of Wellington boots (no pun). I have got a ripping sword & am getting a revolver, & prismatic compass & a pr. of Field glasses; I have resorted to the Exchange & Mart for the latter, they are one of the most difficult things to obtain. Of course I look a fearful knut[1] in uniform, at least 6 friends have already asked for photos, so I suppose I shall have to be taken.

For the first week I was here there was a gale the whole time with rain, now the wind has stopped but we still get rain & the road into Grantham which is about 3 miles is quite 2 inches in mud owing to the traffic on the roads. Last Wednesday our Quartermaster committed suicide. It created quite a sensation, & we got fairly minute details from the doctor in the mess, but no more on the subject.

All Officers have to go on the Square for the first 2 weeks or so, drilling with the recruits or else drilling them which has been my job lately, I can manage them far better than the C.L.B.[2] I think but we shall change when the war is over I think.

I am nearly asleep but if I don't get this done tonight it will have to wait another day as we have no time for writing during the day, although I cannot say we are overworked (that is the recruits). The P.S.U.[3] from which I was discharged will never get to the front as a fighting unit I think as every one is getting or have got Commissions, consequently recruits are always pouring in.

I used to get to Town fairly often and got to several Theatres. I saw 'Drake' (Beerbohm Tree), 'Grumpy' (Cyril Maude), 'Maureen' (Oscar Ashe), 'The Great Adventure' & 'Miss Hook of Holland'; I visited Leonard

---

1 A swell or smart fellow.
2 Church Lads Brigade.
3 Public Schools Unit.

twice and Cousin Maud twice; I also went to the Malvern Mission for one week-end. I suppose everyone saw that Mr Hewetson was blown up with the 'Bulwark' & that Rowley Owen, after going through Mons[4] etc, was wounded in the knee & is at present in the hospital at Boulogne; he is one of the few remaining Officers in this regiment who was at the front & there are hardly any men left out of the battalions which went out, they were practically wiped out as soon as they got there, I hope we keep all their traditions except that of being wiped out. What a day it will be if we all assemble at Pindar Oaks again (if we ever do). Of course Willie and I may meet in Berlin.

There is some likelihood of Christmas leave being stopped I think, as the Germans will think that is just the time for them to come over here when ½ the armies are on leave. At any rate we shall not get more than 2 days which will be any days but Christmas.

I noticed in the Nov. Army List that in one Battln, the East Riding's W. Elmhirst & 2 or 3 others were the only Officers of the Battln. I suppose one acts Colonel the other 2nd in Command & the other Adjutant, & perhaps a couple of subalterns, what fun! I hope when Leonard gets to Town he will carry at least 1d[5] in his pocket, for when I met him in Town, he invariably had nil. or somewhere near, & I had to <u>lend</u> him money for theatre, tea, buses, tubes, chocolates, train fares, papers, cigarettes, drinks, programmes etc. etc., wait till we meet again.

Well Tommy congratulations on your grand performance at the Dardanelles & may a shell never do any more than whistle, if you can't <u>hit</u>, why then, whistle. Many happy returns of your birthday & <u>best wishes for Christmas & 'a appy new year' & I'll try & not forget yer, when I drink a glass 'o beer</u>. See the poetry. Leonard says something about Vic & footer colours. Is it true, well, congratulations on it & on the handkerchief (folded twice). As for Richie, I should think when he

---

4   This was a battle involving the British Expeditionary Force. They inflicted heavy casualties on the Germans, but then had to retire fighting a successful rearguard action.

5   One penny (in old money).

leaves Rugby he'll know every inch of the sick room and San, hurry up and get better. Alfie, I hope the Olive Branch fracture is mended & you have been beaten with something similar to make you a good boy. As for Irene (last but not least) I saw her only 10 days ago, as cheeky as ever.

Well fare the well etc. The Cambdown [sic] Lady sings this song.

Best wishes all from your ever affectionate Brother,

E. Chris. Elmhirst

From Willie.   9th Bn. East York. Regt.
                                Fulford Barracks
                                York.
                                Sunday Dec. 13th 1914.

Dear Leonard etc,

I was quite surprised to get the F.B. back so soon. It's done the first lap in about seven weeks which isn't bad going. But it seems a very long time since I wrote my first contribution & I've changed my address twice since then. My commission was in the Gazette on Oct 23rd, to date from Oct. 20, & I got my orders on the 27th to join the 3rd Bn. E. York. Regt. until the 9th Bn. was formed. So after getting most of my kit I joined at Hedon on Saturday Nov. 7th.

Hedon is a small town about 6 miles East of Hull & 3 miles North of the Paull Battery on the Humber. I was billeted on a man who was Clerk to the Magistrates, an assistant Overseer, acting Clerk for a man who was buying horses for the Army, a Borough Councillor & in charge of the church yard. I received no information of any sort on reporting at Headquarters except that I should probably be sent to York on the Monday, where the 9th was to be formed. On the Sunday night I hunted up the Orderly Room & found that I was down in Orders to go to York at 9.15 on Monday, so it was lucky I went round.

So on the Monday with four other 2nd. Lts. & a Lt. I left for York. At Beverley which, is our Regimental Depot, we picked up 300 men for our Bn. & when we got to York we found our Colonel, Quartermaster & a Lieutenant. On the Wednesday 600 more men arrived from Beverley & another man & I had to go down & fetch them up to Barracks. The first lot had had 10 weeks training but the 600 & another 300 which came on the Saturday had only just enlisted. So for the first week there were 9 Officers to look after 1200 men, most of whom had nothing but what they stood in, the blue serge uniforms, no spare shirts, boots or socks or knives & forks, or razors etc & many of their boots through at the sole. Now at last we have got them all with two pairs of boots & everything except a spare uniform. About 300 have not got the khaki for which they are all longing. We have also got 33 Officers now though all, except the

C.O., the Adjutant & the Quartermaster, are new to the job, though two of our former Captains went through the South African War, but were with Irregular Cavalry Forces and never did any Infantry work.

We are extraordinarily fortunate in having comfortable Barracks instead of huts or billets &, though a week ago we got orders to clear off to Harrogate into billets. We have since been told we may stay here for the present, but if we can get the Grand Hotel at H'gate, which will take both Officers and men, we shall probably move there sometime after Xmas. We have no rifles yet but hope to get them fairly soon. At present, owing to a lack of Senior Officers, I am in a Company with a Lieutenant in command, & am second in command of it & have the first platoon in it (1 platoon = roughly 60 men, I have 70 as 2 cooks, a military policeman, a cobbler and a pioneer are attached to it. 4 platoons = 1 Company, 4 Companies = 16 platoons = 1 Battallion.)

I'll just give you an idea of an ordinary day's work.

6.30	I rise (every day bar Sunday & then 7.30)

7.00	I accompany my Company Officer to Company Orderly Room where offenders are brought up before him to punish or reserve for the Colonel's decision according to their offence. If he is away at any time I shall have to do it. If no offences I have to visit the different rooms (8) to see that all the men are up & dressed.

Breakfast.

8.30 – 12.30	Parade including Squad Drill, Physical Drill, Judging Distance, Visual Training, Rapid Marching, Extended Order Drill, or Saluting Drill & at present a 4 hour march every other day with a 2 hour march in the afternoon on alternate days.

1p.m.	Lunch

2-4	Parade. Drill according to a fixed programme.

4.0	Tea

5.30   A Lecture on different topics from the C.O. or Adjutant to all the Officers.

6.0 – 6.30 or 7. Each platoon Officer lectures his men on some subject such as Discipline, Sanitation, Military Terms, Night Work etc. or else takes them out for Night Work.

Dinner & after that you are supposed to do some reading & you may have all sorts of lists to make out concerning your men & you don't get to bed till 12.0.

I have a book with the name, number & initials of every man in my platoon; whether he is married or single, when he enlisted, how old he is, what his religion is, how many children he has, whether boys or girls, & their ages, what he is giving his wife or anyone else each week out of his pay, what trade he was, & the name and address of his nearest relation, & I may have to fill in more details later.

The first 300 men were a poor lot, mainly Hull loafers or dockhands, but the other 900 are practically all miners from Durham, & a pretty good set of men. Though very thick in the head & very childlike they are all as keen as mustard, though they have not yet got used to the meaning of discipline.

<u>Leonard</u>. No. I didn't use the nose bag when examining the 400 feet of the Company after a four hour route march. It wasn't nearly so bad as smelling 3500 lbs of meat in 100 lb pieces which I had to do the other day, before condemning it to be burned.

<u>Christie.</u> Congratulations on the commission. I'll call yours the D. of W's Regt. If you will call mine the 9th East Yorkshire's or 9th East York. Regt & not East Riding or East Yorks.

<u>Tommy.</u> Congratulations on your shooting. Thanks for your card & best wishes for birthday & Xmas. Hope you have got the baccy pouch by now.

<u>Vic.</u> Congratulations on Colours.

Richard. Hard Lines! Hope you will be right by the time you see this.

Pom. Hope the arm is right, "Remember the greengages" at Xmas.

Irene. A marvellous letter.

At present I'm arranging for 360 lbs of Turkey, oranges & apples & 92 dozen mince pies for Xmas Day dinner for the men. I think it's a good idea to take the letters out at home.

 Much love to you all from your loving brother,

 Willie

My word! What an effort!!

From Richie.   Pindar Oaks, Barnsley.
                                29th December 1914.

Dear Family,

I hope you are all keeping fit as fiddles. I have nearly got to that stage, I came down to breakfast this morning and tidied up the yard and the bantam house working in my great coat. Since last I saw the F.B. nothing special has happened at Rugby, except that I was in bed for 5 weeks and I was practically starved and came home in the motor.

We have won all our matches except one and we are equal cock-house. I pity Leonard when the Budget comes to him; there will only be Tommy's letter as he has seen all the others. The "Rooks", (Uncle Bert etc) have established themselves above us in the "Rookery", where they look very nice!! I have been sleeping in the spare room with a fire, but of course I have to give up my room for the usual, Auntie Frances.

You will have to excuse only 2 pages as four people are writing from home. Irene is no good at keeping things safe. She got a 2/6d knife this morning. She lost it this afternoon while playing chase. We hope she will find it again. We are going on a ratting expedition, tomorrow possibly. No guns, Conus, sticks and ferrets. Leonard is going to Goathland tomorrow. He went to Sheffield today. I cannot find anything to say now unless I say what every body else has said.

A happy new year to everybody from,

Richard Elmhirst.

From Alfred. Pindar Oaks, Barnsley.
29th December 1914.

Dear Tommy. (I mean everybody)

We have all had tea and we three are in the dining room writing a letter to you. We saw your post card's post mark, Queenstown (er-hum) !!! I should think you are having pretty rough weather just now so I will send you a scarf and a pair of cuffs which I knitted myself; if you don't need them you'll be able to find some one else who will I'm sure. I wonder if your Christmas pudding has reached you yet.

I suppose you know that I am going to Winchester. There will be quite a set out of Public Schools: Malvern, Repton, Osbourne, Dartmouth, Marlborough, Rugby and Winchester. My arm is quite alright now only I haven't to be too rough with it. It is ripping, Jack and Cecil living next door to us. We have chases over both gardens. I think we are going out ratting sometime with them, Conus, ferrets, nets, sticks and no guns.

Goodbye now, love to all from your loving brother

Alfred.

Leonard, keeper and I set quite 12 rats out of a nest, all monsters!!

Father rat was the only one that didn't escape, the ferrets killed that!!!!

From Irene Rachel.   Pindar Oaks, Barnsley.
                     29th December 1914.

Dear Didumses,

Hoping you are all in the best of health as I am at preasant. I am none the worse for Christmas festivities. All my stock of beasts are all in health, alive and kicking (hard too). The ferrits are very good now and work like nigers when they go out. I have got three. Daddy is not going to sell any. The misses and Mr Bantys are very well. Vic, Richie and me cleaned them out this morning (I mean their place not them). They have not begun to lay yet, naughty beasts. Down in the field the hens are all very well tho we are only getting one egg a day.

Spider, Doctor, Dartmoor and Pindar are all very well. Doctor's knee is just about all right now and she works hard. She and Dartmoor led hay today. Spider is just as frisky as she used to be, the foal is very dirty and growing hard. Conus is the same naughty, mischievous little rogue. He is allowed in the school-room now for lessons on the hassock where I can pat him now and then.

Vic, Alfie, Jack, Cecil[1] and I had a lovely game of chase this afternoon all over both gardens and we did have fun. Daddy and Mother went up there for lunch today and Leonard was out so us four (Vic, Richie, Alfie and I) had dinner together, it was fine. Chris got leave from Thursday (Christmas eve) to Monday, which was very nice.

Much love from your loving sister,

Irene.

---

1 Jack and Cecil were well liked cousins (sons of Uncle Bert).

From Leonard.	Trinity College
Cambridge
Feb. 10. 1915.

Mei Cari Tutti,

So many complaints have reached me from various quarters that at last I am forced to take pen and write. Lots of things have happened since I put it safely into my box.

I hope you can read this but I am in the train & it is not the Midland railway. Stacks of work to be done & no time to do it all without very careful arrangement.

My numerous activities have more or less confined themselves to working for my exam, but I have taken a YMCA Coll one night a week & am responsible for it. About 200 soldiers came to read, write & sing, & I sell stamps & P.C.'s, play an odd game of draughts or fox & geese, talking to the Families on all kinds of subjects & getting to know them. Tomorrow I sing some of them a duet at a concert a friend of mine has arranged. Being YMCA, no cards are allowed & we always end up with a hymn & prayers. One would like to give one's time to the job, but at present one night a week is all I can manage.

I heard from a man in the Flying Corps today. If any of you want to get in I can tell you how. Learning is not more than twice as difficult as riding a bicycle. After 3 weeks you take your "plane" up alone & then fly continuously. There have been only 18 casualties in the Flying Corps up to January.

I spent last weekend in Oxford & had a fine time. It's a lively place as Willie will tell you & has lots of things which I much envy, especially its lovely old streets, beautifully wide, & hardly a new house to be seen, very like what it was 300 years back I should think.

This week end Christie has spent with me, I managed to keep him busy. Dinner with one don & two officers, lunch with another. An entirely home cooked breakfast which he could not stop grumbling about in spite of a first class omelette.

Congratulations to Tommy & Willie. One has 1st Lieut & Christie on being in the Colonel's good books. Vic on writing me a letter, Richie on not being ill & Pom on being at Winchester, you are a lucky boy, Irene on her peremptory p-c.

Yr affect. Br,

L.K.E.

From Christie.   8th D. of W's
                                  Belton Park
                                  Grantham
                                  Saturday Feb. 13. 1915

My dear All

How nice it is to see the F.B. again, but as it has stayed in Leonard's hands such a long time, I'm afraid the news is all rather old. I saw Leonard last week-end, he gave me quite a decent time; I think I only had 3 meals with him, his chief fault was not enough to eat at breakfast (or drink).

Well since I wrote last in the F.B. many things have occurred. As you all know I have a Platoon now which, by the way, I have not seen for a week, as I have been taking a course of lectures with 3 others of this Regt from one Colonel Malcolm who is 'fresh from the front' & very interesting. He is a Brigadier and knows what he is talking about; we have had 3 days in doors having lectures, & enlarging maps & 3 days outside using the maps we have made & putting more things on. To day has been very wet, I went out without a coat & came back soaked through about 6 times. As you all know I <u>was</u> junior Subaltern of this Battln, but a week ago I found myself 3rd out of 12 2nd Lts., the other 6 being promoted.

A few days ago the Adjutant told me I was to be a machine gun officer. There are 2 M. gun officers in a Battalion, each in command of 1 section which is composed of 2 guns, & as you all know we reckon rounds of ammunition by the 100, we manage about 300 rounds per minute. So, in the course of a few days I shall throw up my Platoon for good to learn how to use a machine gun. An Officer called 'Ince' has just arrived, he was at the Front with Rowley Owen until he had to come home owing to illness. He tells many tales & says that if anyone gets killed, it is the M. Gun Officer because, as soon as the M.G. is spotted, it is shelled by artillery & infantry; so that is a lively look-out for me.

I've been in charge of the Company (250) quite a lot now & one day took Orderly Room. There was (unfortunately) only 1 prisoner & I admonished him, he must have been pleased. Next week, Feb 14-20, we do Brigade training, that is 4000 men training together in field operations. We went billeting one night at the end of January. I got to a lovely house but unfortunately could only spend from 4.30 am to 6.30 in bed as I went round the billets from 10 p.m. to 12 & then from 12 to 4 am we formed an 'Outpost' line in front of the village Long Bennington to prevent attack on our troops from the enemy which was not there. I was in charge of about 60 men (1 picquet etc.) We were stationed on the G. North Road between Grantham & Newark; I tried to sleep (1) where the stone heap <u>had been</u> & (2) where the stone heap <u>was</u>, but the night being such an awfully cold one it was impossible to sleep & I could not walk about over much.

Another day we set off to some trenches about 6 miles away at 4 o'clock. We got there at 6 (pitch dark) took the place off another Regiment who had commenced them, improved them & returned back at 10.30 pm, getting in about 12.15 a.m. We set off again next morning at 8 am, examined the trenches by daylight & then filled them in, we had our lunch cooked in the field, & very good it was, & returned back about 4 o'clock feeling rather tired.

Last night we had a concert in our own dining hall with a sketch at the end based on the song, 'Sister Suzy sewing shirts for soldier's'! I sang 'The Twin Duet' with another fellow & we were loudly cheered & whistled, but owing to the large programme there was no time for them. I sang 'Old Shako'[1] which went quite well, in fact I believe it was encored. Then I changed again for 'Sister Suzy'; I was Suzy & since last night have been complimented many times as to what a lovely lady I made, & so I did. Marjorie had sent me a beautiful costume which looked very nice, at least I thought so, but another Officer bought a very fashionable one which did not fit him & fitted me better than Marjorie's so I wore it. One remark overheard this morning was, "It were a fine show, but Mr Elmhirst, eh, 'e made a champion lass". We are going to try & keep a thing like this going once a fortnight.

Well, I hope to get home next Saturday, Feb 20. all being well. Willie will soon be a bloomin' Capn. I expect we'll hope so. Congratulations

---

1 Old Shako and Sister Suzy were popular songs of the time (see internet).

to Leonard on managing to scrawl 3 sheets, but he ought to send an interpreter with it; I wonder if we shall all see Tommy again shortly, let's hope so. I suppose Vic will soon be thinking of taking a Commission at least in 2 or 3 years. I suppose Richie is at Grange now having a gay old time, and Alfie is piling on the 'swank' at Winchester. He'd better be padded when he comes home. I hope the birds beasts & animals are not all empty with the 'cleaning out' that Irene seems to be giving them. Congrats to myself on not yet having kept this budget more than one day.

Well good-bye all from your affectionate brother,

E. Chris. Elmhirst

From Willie.　　　　　　　　　　Imperial Hydro Hotel,
　　　　　　　　　　　　　　　　Hornsea
　　　　　　　　　　　　　　　　March 24th 1915.

Dear Family

First of all I must apologise for keeping the F.B. for over a month. I have been very busy but might have found time if only I hadn't kept forgetting it. Quite a lot has happened since last I wrote & probably you have most of you heard about it. My last letter was written on Dec. 13th.

Then I got my Xmas leave from Jan 7 – Jan 11. On Jan 29th I was gazetted full Lieutenant to date from Jan 7th, quite a pleasant birthday present, & on Jan 12th I was made President of the Mess Committee which meant I had the running of the Officers Mess, arranging for & paying servants, ordering & paying for stuff & in fact housekeeping for between 45 and 50 Officers, making out their bills at the end of each month & seeing that they were all paid. The food bills from tradesmen usually come to about £150 a month, & one day when I spent an hour in the town paying for them I spent money at the rate of 23/- a minute for that hour! However I've finished with that job now I'm glad to say, as we have a second in command now, & it is a job which the 2nd in command always has to look after. I handed everything over four days ago.

On Feb. 2nd I was made 2nd in command of my Company which is a job a Capt. has in the Regular Army, so it was a pretty good rise for me. I no longer have a platoon to look after but have to help my Company Commander to look after the whole show and if he is away I have to do it by myself.

You may be wondering what I'm doing at Hornsea. I arrived here the day before yesterday with another Lt & 2 2nd/Lts. from the 9th to go through a course of instruction for a month. There are 85 of us altogether from dozens of different Regiments & they've got some Regular Officers here who are trying to teach us as much as possible in the time so we are doing some real hard work. The hours are 9 to 1 in the morning & 2 to 5 & 6 – 7 in the afternoon, so we are doing 8 solid hours a day which includes 2 hours lectures. Tomorrow afternoon we are spending three hours in digging trenches & are going to be in canvas suits all day long. They give us each a suit of canvas so as not to get our uniforms filthy. We do an hours physical training at present every morning first thing which warms you up considerably.

We occupy the whole Hotel which has been taken over by the War Office & so are fairly comfortable. Some people are two in a room but I have quite a nice one to myself. There's a large sea water swimming bath downstairs which is to be heated for us. It wasn't this morning and after one length I got out feeling perfectly numb it was so cold. We are only to be charged 1/- a week for the use of it, which isn't much.

By the time we have finished here, our Battalion is to be under canvas near Harrogate or Lichfield. We don't know which yet, but we move in on the 15th of next month.

Our 2nd in command of the 9th who has just come is an awfully good man. He was mentioned in despatches thirteen times in the South African War & was publicly thanked before an army for his work by Kitchener. He got a C.M.G. & D.S.O. for it. He's a Lieut. Col & it's the first time he's been in England for 27 years.

I had a visit from Tommy on his first bit of leave after the action in the North Sea[1] & then got home for a weekend the second time he was at home.

Tommy. Congratulations on your rise in prospects, pay, & position and thanks for your letter. I'll try to answer it sometime soon. You're the millionaire of the family now.

Leonard. Hope you get a lot of reading done & in case I don't get F.B. before Schools, the best of luck & a first in them or should I say a 1.1.

Christie. Nothing for you as I've just seen you, also

---

1 The battle of the Dogger Bank when brother Tommy was a midshipman on HMS Indomitable which sank the German battle cruiser SS Blucher.

Irene. but I hope she has got Conus better.

Vic. Hope your cold is all right again. Sorry you didn't win the Hurdles.

Richie. Hope you're keeping fit.

Pom. Hope you know all your notions by now.

I suppose there'll be a whacking apiece between the three of you before the end of term.

I got home for last weekend, Saturday morning to Monday afternoon, saw all the relations & had a good game of golf at Wortley on Monday morning with Daddy.

Love to you all from your loving but excessively busy brother,

Willie

P.S. The 5th Bn. York. & Lancs. came to York a fortnight ago so I've seen cousin Jim, (3 or 4 times to talk to) George Hewitt and Hugh Raley.

From Christie.

8th D. of W's
Belton Park
Grantham
3/4/15

Dear All

I hope this will reach you by Sunday morning; I wish I could too, but I can't so there's an end of it. I wish you all a very happy Easter. I hope there will be a good family gathering, & mind, at lunch to give mother a glass of port to drink the health of '<u>poor</u> Tommy, <u>in the air</u>'. We are all up to the top half of our heads in work. It is no small job packing up everything in the battalion. I don't know whether you have a <u>good</u> map of England, (Willie had one once, a cycling map) but I will tell you the way we are going.

Depart Grantham – Monday morning arrive Waltham on the Wold near Melton Mowbray Monday night, April 5th/6th arrive Rearsby Tuesday night 6th/7th Wednesday we pass through Leicester & billet at Cosby 7th/8th

Thursday – billet at Gilmorton near Lutterworth 8th/9th & on Friday we entrain at Lutterworth for Witley & there until further notice all letters for me can be addressed [address then crossed out] see last sheet.

I've done nothing this week of much importance except pass the elementary Machine Gun test which was very easy; I got 100%, about 3 others got it too. We have had a nice fine week until Good Friday when rain started & now it is pouring & has been all day. Let me warn you before hand, especially Daddy to whom they are addressed, that I have this day despatched one packing case by goods Rly. & on Monday I shall have despatched a hand bag (Willie's) & a Gladstone (mine), both empty, they will come Passenger. I am also sending home all my bills (don't get frightened) which are paid, I wonder if Daddy can keep them for me, also one empty cheque book. Oh, I may send a parcel home with a few dirty clo' I don't want & some oddments including a little broach that may do for Irene, also the key of my Gladstone. This is all jolly interesting to everyone I'm sure, at any rate it helps to fill.

I suppose Leonard has returned stony broke as usual, I hope Mother is at home for Easter & that Pom is better. Through leaving my vest off I have had a cold this week but now it is better & I have all the less to carry, so it was worth it. I've just been down to Grantham for the last time with 4 other Subalterns; we have nearly bought Grantham up between us I think. I am sending a couple of photos (which please return), just to show you what a few of my fellow-Officers look like. The centre one (Mulholland) has sprained his ankle.

Well, I really think I must stop. Oh, rumour's latest is that we go to the Dardanelles in a fortnight, I hope it may be true. We had a service yesterday & the rest of the day did nothing but I'm afraid to-morrow will not be a day of rest for any of us Officers as we have all got some job on. Well good-bye all from

E. Chris. Elmhirst

My address will be

8th D. of W's
11th Division
Witley Gamp
Godalming
Guildford
Surrey

From Vic.   Preshute House,
                                            Marlborough.
                                            9th May 1915.

My Dearest's,

All the usual and unusual excuses for sending the F.B. off too soon. I made a large mistake when I took it home to write in the holidays as it is nearly impossible to write it then. Anyhow I have beaten Willie and Leonard etc. It seems both possible and easy now to imagine Willie and Christie Generals and Tommy as Admiral from what I have heard about them.

Congratulations to Christie for looking like Suzy. I believe Tommy did the same sort of thing at Dartmouth didn't he. I suppose Willie will have soon finished the musketry course at York and will have to try to instruct his company and battalion. I hope Tommy will have good luck and will spot and destroy lots of submarines. I wonder if he has used the thermos yet and whether he is thinking of flying home some day soon, also whether he has procured his pay and how much it is. To Leonard, best wishes for his coming exam. I have been thinking of giving you the £40 or so to get you the M.A!!! From the amount of work we let you do in the holidays I think you will easily fail to get a 3rd.

Last holidays we had a good day at Wortley. I got only 2 crows eggs, but 16 hens eggs for tea. The motor was unlucky but still we got on all right. I expect you all have heard this before, but one or two may not. I am in a kind of preparation class now and hope to get into the Army Class next term and from thence to Woolwich in 2 or 3 terms we will hope.

I had a good journey down here at the beginning of the term though very hot, but it passed quickly as I had a book. On the evening of that day I went a 2 mile ride on the carrier of our house captain's bike, a 2 cylinder Douglas and we got up to 40 m.p.h. It was a bit bumpy but nice and exciting and there were no accidents. We are having delightful weather, but have not started bathing yet. I have been a few good rides two or three times. One was 42 miles in the afternoon. It is a preparation for going to Stonehenge which is 50.

I have managed to get a promo in Form and Stinks and in Mr Hewitt's (Old Dog's) Form, which is Modern Upper I and in Mr Alsopp's (Sloppy's) Stinks set.

I heard a cuckoo for the first time a few days ago and that day an aeroplane came over and dropped a note for one of the masters. We were working at the time, but went to the window to see it. I do not know how you can write about 8 pages. I can only do about half that.

To Alfie. I hope you have learned your notions by now. I wonder if your "Tije"[1] has been turned up yet. We had a night attack last night. It started about 7.10. Then we had a practice attack on the Downs till it got dark and then the real one. It was rather cold and we had to be absolutely silent, but it was great fun, especially the march home when we sang hard the whole time. We got into bed about 11.00 and our House Master was awfully fed up as he hadn't been told we were even going to have it. We had to get upstairs with anything we had and jump into bed immediately. Not even a wash!! We were in a nice state but I managed to get a good bath in the morning.

To Richie. In about a week you will receive a couple of shirts from me, but at present I am wearing one and the other is in the wash.

Much love to all and sundry of the scattered family from your affectionate brother,

Vic.

---

1 Tégé was the name for the commoners house at Winchester. It is pronounced "teejay," but here Vic puns the word with 'tie.'

From Richie. 4 Horton Crescent, Rugby.
10th May 1915.

Dear WLCTVRAI etc etc.

It's a long way to Tip – sorry, I meant it's a long time since I saw the F.B. I hope you are all alright. It's not long since I saw you all. I went to Coumes[1] the day after Vic went and had to do all the climbing by myself. The first tree was easy, contents of nest; 5 eggs and a "babs", as Irene says. Second nest; beastly. An old beech slippery with rain, but the products, 5 eggs. Coming down, tore a large hole in my trousers. Then we had lunch. Then Irene and I set off to a nest above the white cottage, rather a beast, but we got 7 eggs!! Then we toiled cross-country to the road where the lane from the barn joins the road.

Another beast of a tree I got up a good way, a swarm of 15 feet and the bird flew off, but I was absolutely done and could not do another inch so we went home with 17 eggs and a babs, which is in a thrushes nest. Irene will tell you about it.

Uncle Harry and Auntie Vin arrived in state on a ripping motor bike and side-car and we had a game of golf on Wednesday. On Thursday, my birthday, (15) we went to Sheffield to take me for my train. Mother, Uncle Harry and Auntie Vin then left me to go to Rotherham. I went to my platform where I found three or four other men going to Rugby.

There has been a cat in our study during the hols having a lovely time making a nest in our 8 cushions, which were piled on a chair. The whole study smells of CAT and all the cushions are covered with hair. Two dachshund puppies have been added to the establishment in place of the other, which came to an untimely end. One is light brown and the other brown-black.

We had our first game of cricket on Saturday. I did not do badly. We have had very good weather lately and the "tosh" (swimming bath)

---

1 Coumes was one of three small tenanted farms near Stocksbridge, about 10 miles from Barnsley. The other two were Foldrings and Bitholmes. (see map)

was opened yesterday afternoon. On Saturday Nan[2] had Marjorie, Mrs Alderson and Mrs Agatha West to lunch and tea. I saw them at Chapel yesterday afternoon. I think they were going on their tour to day. I think we might do a record now and try and get it round a little quicker. I know Leonard is working very hard.

<u>Willie</u>. Congratulations on passing the musketry test. I hope you will settle somewhere soon.

<u>Leonard.</u> I hope you will do well in your exam. You ought to after all the little excitements at the schoolroom window during the hols to wake you up.

<u>Christie.</u> Come up to Rugby again soon.

<u>Tommy.</u> Get to work as soon as possible. I hope the bike is alright.

<u>Vic.</u> I hope you will get to Stonehenge and back. Use more lickey on your envelope, it came unstuck.

<u>Pom.</u> Send the F.B. on fairly soon, unless the "tegeing" is still going on. I hope you won't have to score so much.

<u>Irene.</u> Don't kick Miss C too hard when in the tent. I hope Conus's little animals have disappeared. He is not quite safe.

Your affectionate brother,

Richard Elmhirst.

---

2 Nan his cousin, was married to his Rugby housemaster, Charles Hawkesworth.

From Alfred.	Chernocke House,
	Winchester.
	12th May 1915.

Dear Fraters and Soror.

Thank you for all your contributions to the F.B. I am afraid I am too busy to get it off immediately, but it only arrived on May 11th afternoon and as it was a half holiday I had to play cricket all the afternoon till 5 o'clock, I am wicket keeper for the game second from bottom, and played for a cap yesterday (Tuesday) letting one bye. I made 4 not out in the first innings and 8 not out in the second.

I am not allowed to go to Gunner's Hole, our bathing place, for a good time after it starts which is rather rotten. It is Ascension Day tomorrow so a whole holiday which is rather nice. There are three leave out days this half and one other whole holiday. My div-don[1] is Mr A.E.Wilson (Archie), my mathematics don is Mr A.E.Broomfield (Bertie) and my French don is Mr Jackson (the Jaquers).

Rockley Wilson is in great form. He bowled to me at nets on Monday 10th May. Altogether I have been getting on very well at work and games.

<u>Willie.</u> I have not been beaten yet, so don't know what a "ground ash" is like.

<u>Leonard.</u> Dearest Grandpa,[2] I hope you'll have the bestest success in your 'books'.

<u>Christie.</u> Hope you will have better luck than is prophesied, and remember to bring me a German helmet.

<u>Tommy.</u> Hope you will run a 'Zep' down one of these days.

<u>Vic.</u> Don't be more of a pig than you can help, or else. Well, wait and see.

---

1 Division don or form master.
2 Leonard was often referred to as "Grandpa" by his younger siblings.

Richie. I wonder how you are getting on in 'Crockets'.

Irene. The usual questions, how are:- Conus, chickens, Tory, horses, bants and everything else I have forgotten.

Ascension Day, a whole holiday and pouring with rain when everyone had settled where to go and what to do. There are some lovely ices here which are nice for a hot day. I was going to play cricket today, but there is no hope for it now. It is nearly dinner time so I must stop. Any contributions to my 'Toyes' will be gratefully received. Well, good-bye me dears, best of luck from your loving brother.

Alfred Octavius Elmhirst.

From Irene Rachel.   Pindar Oaks, Barnsley.
                                      26th May 1915.

Dear Didumses,

I hope you are all all right. I am "still going strong", so is the farm yard. There is one new addition to the horses which you have all heard about, the foal, and Chris and Tommy have seen. He (the foal) is light brown just now with two white socks right up to his knees in front and one small white sock behind. He has a brown mane and brown tail with some white in it and tries to kick Henry if he pats him on the back. Spider is very good and lets anyone go to her. I have been out a lot already. Doctor is lovely and looks fine in her new summer coat. Chris rode her quite a lot when he came home. Dartmoor is very well and of course very fat. Pindar is quite alright, but has not got his summer coat yet.

The chickens are all right, but I am having rather bad luck with them, for one thing, Tony[1] the bad wretch has eaten four chicks and one bant. I found him in the kennel with the tail and two legs of one chicken sticking out of his mouth. The ferrets are very well. On Saturday, a very hot day, I found Mr ferret lying down on the floor of the hutch with his hind legs out behind him and his front ones in front of him and his tongue lolling out, he did look funny. I gave him some water and Mrs. I put a mackintosh over them (not over them, but over the hutch). The bants are very well. The little bantys have flying practice and they like it I am sure, though I have not asked them!!

Miss Coleclough[2] and I go to the swimming baths tomorrow. It's only the second time so far. She did not go in last time as she wanted to watch, but she is going in this time and [will] have a lesson I expect. The old baths now have a water chute so they are just about as good as the new ones and some good diving boards. I dived from the deep end last time and I am going off one of the diving boards this time.

---

1 Tony was the family spaniel.
2 Miss Coleclough was Irene Rachel's governess at the time.

Tony is not rid of the ----------------------- I won't say what!!! But Conus[3] does not catch any now I am sure and Tommy and Chris have had him sleeping in their rooms. Chris did not have him on his bed, but Tommy did as he had just been washed. I washed Conus twice in a week a little time ago for rolling. He is a very ill-mannered little dog.

Miss Coleclough's and my room have been papered. Mine is sweet peas and looks topping. Miss Coleclough's is a sort of mixture. I have got Willie's and Christie's swords now and Tommy's dirk to hang up. We had the Worsbro Dale and Worsbro Common children on Whit Monday. They had a very good time, so did I too. Daddy got an ice cream man to come, a very nice one, so of course we had to try the ices. Daddy had one (he was having two only Marjorie had the other). Mother had one, Miss C two and Chris four and me six. They only went a very little way too. The man got 2s-4d. just with half pennys, pretty good.

On Tuesday St Johns children came. I only had one ice then. We did not do anything for them, but for the others, we turned ropes for skipping, got races up, played all sorts of games and I did work hard. I used more than a shilling in giving prizes for skipping and races and did them myself too. They're jolly hard to do too because about a dozen children gather round you and shout and hold up their hands and it's rather hot work, but great fun.

May 27th. Miss Coleclough and I have just been to the swimming baths, but she did not go in as she had a headache or something. I had a lovely time and went down the water chute about a dozen times. Last Saturday Daddy had to go to his dentist so Chris went with him and Mother and I. While Daddy was at the dentist the motor was put up at Clark's where Tommy's motor bike is and I saw it. It's a lovely one. Mother and I stopped while Chris got his hair cut, then Mother went into a Hotel near Clark's and wrote letters to Pom and Leonard. I think I had some ginger beer. Then Chris came back and he and I went to look for Daddy and did a little shopping and got some topping flowers for Mother and, of course, sweets for me!! (Chris said that the Hotel Mother went to in Doncaster was a Public House - as he called it.)

---

3 Conus was the family terrier (and rat catcher).

On Monday Daddy Chris and I and Dr Fryer went to Wortley golfing. It was hot, but we had very good fun. You will all have heard of George[4] of Elmhirst, that he has died. Daddy and I went up there yesterday and poor Rover was sitting on the doorstep looking so pathetic. He just came a few yards to lick Daddy's hand and my legs and then went back to the doorstep. His feet are very bad and he can only walk a few yards and then he drags himself along. Naughty Conus of course wanted to fight him and would have done him as he is too weak to fight. We have got a lot of rooks from Elmhirst, about 29 or more and Miss Coleclough liked "Pigeon" pie very much!! As we had to call it.

Willie. I have cleaned out the bants house, not them this time, so mind what you say.

Leonard. I expect you will be getting a 1st in your exam with the working you did here. Do you remember having shots at my hand out of the schoolroom window!!!

Chris. I have just seen you. I hear you only just caught the train at Doncaster.

Tommy. I only saw you on Monday. Bad Conus has just rolled this morning and Mother watched him out of her window rolling in the field with great relish!!

Vic. Your bike will be the same old bone-shaker soon by your stories about your bike rides. You will want a new outer and inner tyre, I should think, after the other one.

Richie. Your cat looks lovely on my mantle piece.

Pom. I hope you have got your bike now.

From your loving sister

Irene.

---

4 George lived in an old cottage behind the Victorian house known as Elmhirst. The cottage has a cruck frame and is believed to have been an ancient residence of the Elmhirsts of Worsbrough.

From Tommy.

Naval Airship Station,
Walney Island,
Barrow-in-Furness.
29th May 1915

My Dears.

The F.B. arrived here today after an extraordinary long absence. I am writing by return, an example which I hope will be closely followed this round.

Since my last contribution I have "shifted billet" twice but I think you know most of my doings up to a month ago. I left Kingsworth on the 15th of this month to come up here as, owing to the slow progress of the airship building down there, they proposed building some up here so six of us were despatched up here of which I am the senior. On the same day I "shipped my first stripe" having been promoted Act. Sub. Lt. RN. This has nothing to do with the RNAS[1] and is my proper Navy promotion.

I bought my motor bicycle about a week before. A 3½ Brooklands model, last years Rudge, Christie, Richie and Irene have already seen it. I meant to ride up to Barrow on it as I had the weekend off stopping the nights at Rugby and home. I started all right with my belongings in a cardboard box in the back of the carrier, but before I had gone ten miles, about 8.30am, I felt behind and found the bottom of the box and a hair brush, then I went back another mile and met a little girl who said a lady had picked them up and taken them to a house, so I went there and recovered them all. I then got up to London and it happened again only not so bad as a shaving brush was the only thing that dropped out and which another lady picked up and gave me when I stopped; I stayed an hour in London and then got up to Rugby in time for a late lunch. I spent 24 hours there and left at 2 pm Sunday for home. I came along at about 30 miles an hour most of the way doing the 30 miles between Leicester and Newark in under an hour. I got to Doncaster by 5 pm, filled up there, got five miles out and then the thing went wrong, magneto armature burnt out, so I left it in a farm yard at Hickleton and another fellow on a motor bike very kindly brought me back to Barnsley.

---

1 Royal Naval Air Service, to which Tommy had been transferred after selection by Admiral Fisher.

I went back there in the car next morning, brought a man in from Charle's garage who wheeled it back! and then came on to Barrow. It is a very good place here within 25 miles of Windermere, I have been there four times and we live in lodgings, four in one house and two in the next one to it, and have quite an amusing time. My own airship which is the first one being built here is progressing favourably though slowly owing to lack of materials, but with luck I should have it ready next week ie the end of the first week in June. At present we have only one thing that flies here, the old army airship Beta, she is nearly on the scrap heap, but she is useful for practice and getting experience in the air. I was home again at the beginning of this week as I had to go to Wakefield to get some wire so put in two nights at home.

My best wishes to you all from your ever affect, brother,

Tommy

From Leonard. Trinity College,
Cambridge.
90 minutes after my
exam on June 2. 1915.

My dear "grandchildren"

You cannot think how it pleased your old grandfather to receive the F.B. the day before his examination. As you see by the above date my last exam is over & here I am lying in a punt of the river, nearly exhausted. I like to think my last exam is over forever, but one never knows.

I've been writing so hard that now I don't know what to say. I think I've got thro. I hope I've got a 2nd, that remains to be seen, but I know most of the examiners (personally I mean). I'm thinking of giving them a party with crackers, it might help. I've just called up three hens and a dog by copying a fowl. I don't (no I've said that once). I've got a new tent you will be glad to hear, & a magnificent sleeping bag.

A new start here, it being Friday evening June 5. Many things have happened since I last took my pen. Yesterday afternoon I went a 28 mile ride with my Director of Studies, a Trinity Fellow, we had a splendid time. Back by 6.30 and into a canoe with another man + <u>the new tent</u>. In my old rucksack was – the tent, an eiderdown sleeping bag, a ground sheet, a canteen, aluminium for two, a Primus spirit stove the present of the family, a woolley waistcoat, sponge, etc, a fireplace, matches pyjamas & the water bottle with milk in. Outside was one tin with food in, & one rug, & mackintosh, the other man also had a rug & mac. We paddled away, only Irene has been I think, of the family, right up the river, hauled the canoe up to banks where there were lock gates & arrived at a suitable place, 2 miles away, no one to be seen, at 8.30, stars beginning to come out. We did have a job, luckily it was a lovely night, & we got the tent up somehow. It has points over the old one, but is not aired well at the top & is not quite so wide but of course about 1/8th of the weight.

Tent up we lit a fire. I confess that, greatly to my shame, we had to use just a wee drappie of paraffin. But it was dark, we had a lovely blaze, & the water was soon simmering on the fire. In another place was the fry pan with bacon, & water hens' eggs (we gathered some 15 on the way up, in the process of breaking them into the pan, in the nick of time, three were found to be, shall we say, well developed eggs), cocoa, bacon & eggs, brown bread & butter, cake & bananas, we <u>were</u> hungry.

Then in we turned. Not a good night. I was v. comfortable, but the tent did not air well & I had to put my head outside. Horses too snorted in our ears. About 2 am there was a great wrench at the tent (a cow) – a few drops fell at one time, more excitement, still a bathe & breakfast soon put it right. It was v. warm and ideal morning. Buttered eggs, hen species this time, kidneys & bacon, oh so good, cocoa, bread & marmalade, & apples. Why the Ritz couldn't have done it better. We had a fire & the roaring primus going, so we only took 2 hours over breakfast. By that time it was v. hot, & we packed up & got aboard. Paddled down about finding a long tailed tit's nest, one egg & some young ducks on the way. It was hot when we came to the 1st lock & had a <u>lovely</u> bathe. Then home for lunch, I drank 2 jugs of lemonade, & have played tennis since. I expect Christie here tomorrow, & one of the Pym family. My Director, a most critical man, is v. encouraging & says I might get a two one, & should get a two two, the other possibilities are a one, & a third, & a plough.

My vac is unsettled at present, also my future. I <u>may</u> go to India for a year before coming up here again, I ought to have said, "I want to". Next weekend I spend perhaps down at Lancing, with a master there, then back here for a degree, L.K.E. B.A. Hons, can't you see me, rabbit skin trailing behind. Well, well, this must end.

Best luck to the warriors, tight lines & all that.

Yr affectionate brother,

L.KE.

From Christie.　　　　　　　　8th D. of W.'s,
　　　　　　　　　　　　　　　Witley Camp,
　　　　　　　　　　　　　　　Surrey.
　　　　　　　　　　　　　　　Monday June 7th 1915.

My dear brothers, etc.

At last after a long journey all over the country, the famous F.B. arrives at my address & I doubt if I should have got it yet, if I hadn't been over to see that fellow Leonard (perhaps you know him) and brought it back with me. I went there for his birthday June 6th. I got to his rooms for lunch; he was playing tennis but left a note telling me to have lunch & go & watch him! Like Old Mother Hubbard, I found the cupboards bare, & all I could find was one small hard week old crust of brown bread, 1 apple & banana & some water, he had finished everything else. Well, I did my duty & soon found him & after quite a good week end I came back here to the hard life of the Army & to hear a few more exciting rumours.

I will take you all on a 'wager' (Mother doesn't like the 3 letter word) that I am not here by the time that the F.B. arrives here again; the wager is that if I am not here you each send me a letter, & if I am here I send you each a letter, that's fair enough. We are living a very strenuous life now, nearly always having a 2 days operation, with the night in the open, bivouacking. It is jolly nice when fine but unpleasant when wet. Then we usually manage a night attack or attack at dawn which are no fun & perhaps one other field day in the week. The rest of my time is taken up in instructing 12 men in the art of the Machine Gun. I am always certain of a horse when I go out on field days now as only one of us goes out, the other stays in to teach, I have a ripping little horse who goes like smoke. We are having awfully hot weather now & we get fearfully fed up occasionally, but a trip to Town bucks one up tremendously.

So far I have stayed with Cousin Lily once, Mrs Fry (Miss Davies) once & have seen Cousin Maud quite a lot; I have been to several excellent theatres & have succeeded in spending a nice bit of money. I happened to be in London on the night of the 1st Air Raid, but I saw nothing on coming out of the theatre at 11.15 p.m. 8 of us left here by 2 motors at

6.30, motored to Town (30 miles), then theatre & dinner afterwards, then back again at 2.30 a.m.

<u>Willie</u>: I foresee a Captaincy coming to you. I hope you may have the best of luck.

<u>Leonard</u>: Get more food for visitors & don't rely on next door neighbours feeding you. Best of luck in your plans.

<u>Christie</u>: Oh, that's me, I forgot.

<u>Tommy</u>: I hope the bike is mended & you have good luck with the baby Zeps.

<u>Vic</u>: More licky on <u>more</u> letters please as Richard says. I hope you reach Stonehenge before you're an old man.

<u>Richie</u>: I'm afraid Rugby is off the books now, but be a good boy & all that sort of thing.

<u>Alfred</u>: I hope you know your notions well & have been beaten well at least once. I might see you before I go.

<u>Irene</u>: Rolling Stones gather no moss

" Conus " ! ! ! ! ! Look after him, the foal, the chickens, & the tea table (from Tony).

Well, this must end; I think 2 weeks from now will see me elsewhere, & I hope so too. A nice little wound after a month to last about 3 months will suit well. Don't try sending the F.B. to me, if abroad, it will most probably get lost.

Your affectionate brother,

E. Chris Elmhirst.

From Willie.

9th E.Y.R.
Killinghall Camp,
Harrogate.
12.35.p.m.
June 12th 1915.

To all whom it may concern, greeting

Quite pleased to see my old friend Mr.F.B.Udget again. On looking at his visiting list I find he stayed nearly six weeks the last time he came to see me. However I'm too busy to spend much time on him now so he's leaving me shortly, probably tomorrow. His travelling expenses must be pretty heavy. Again I write from different quarters & again I have undergone changes. Since our last number I have spent 2 fortnights at the School of Musketry at Strensall near York, one a Rifle Course at which I qualified "with distinction" as an Instructor in Musketry & the other a Machine Gun Course at which I qualified as an Instructor in Machine Guns, and now I have finished up as M.G. Officer to the Battalion.

At present with 4 other M.G. Officers of different Battalions in our Brigade here, we are carrying on a School of Instruction in M.G.'s & training 10 Officers & 20 N.C.O.'s in M.G. work. We start work at 6.45 every morning & do an hour then, then 9 to 12.30 & 2 to 4.30. The Course lasts a fortnight & I give 3 lectures to the whole lot, an hour each & the others each give some. Then we have to examine the class, which is divided into squads. I have 2 Officers & 4 Sergeants in mine. Now for lunch, 1.0 p.m. & at 2.0 I ride about 6 miles to Starbeck for golf with Uncle Harry.

<u>Sunday</u> 5.45. Had a very good game with Uncle H. & beat him & he, Aunt Vin & I had tea at the Clubhouse after it. Then they went home and I returned my borrowed clubs to the Guy family & stopped there for supper. I'm taking two people there for tennis tomorrow evening. Today after Church Parade (about 5000 of us) I walked into Harrogate & had lunch with Mrs Kemble. Then about 3.0 I went to Cousin Fanny's – Mrs. Crowe – & had a hot bath, then I came back here for tea as she & her beloved who is on leave from our 3rd Battalion were going out for tea.

Three of our nicest officers, two of them pals of mine went out to the Mediterranean three weeks ago & we are afraid one has been wounded as the C.O. has had a wire from the War Office asking for his next of kin's address. I should probably have gone by now as I was in the first four on the list of those who were ordered to be ready to go any moment, only the C.O. wrote to the War Office to ask if he could keep me back, so now I'm probably a fixture for the next two or three months. However everyone will probably get out sooner or later. We're rather short of tents here so officers are 3 to a tent which doesn't leave much room to spare.

It's quite pleasant in this sort of weather to jump out of your flea bag into a cold bath just outside your tent at 6.0 a.m. though there was quite a cool breeze this morning. Oswald Guy was at home from last Sunday till Thursday for his four days leave. I got some tennis with him last Monday. Our Colonel has just left us & gone to the Leeds Bantams, so for the present our 2nd in command is in charge, but I believe a new C.O. is coming this week. We've got a man here now as a 2nd. Lt. who was a pre. at Malvern when I first went there. I used to fag for him & he left about 3 years before I did. Now it's the other way round except that he doesn't fetch my boots for me as I used to do for him.

<u>Leonard</u> Hope you've got your double one. You might look me up before you go to India. You'll be as great a traveller as Tommy soon. Hope you'll have a good time if you go. I told Uncle Harry when I was over at Ark[1] that you might go.

<u>Christie</u> Best of luck. The (bet) is on. Did Leonard borrow any money from you in addition to starving you when you went over to see him.

<u>Tommy</u> I suppose you've got your wings now & your bike. Mine's going as well as ever.

<u>Vic</u> Got measles yet? "On what did the Stonehinge hinge?" I'll give anyone sixpence who sends the right answer.

<u>Richard</u> Any more "catastrophes" lately? Try a cat-apult. Hope you've not cat-ched any diseases this term. Many happy returns.

---

1 His Uncle Harry lived at Arkendale.

<u>Alfred</u> I'll show you my ground-ash next time we meet if you like. It wants exercise.

<u>Irene</u> What was it I found on Conus last time I went home? I won't tell the others. But <u>I</u> didn't have him on <u>my</u> bed.

Much love to Everyone from your loving brother

Leonard's great grandfather

A RECORD

From Vic.　　　　　　　　　　Preshute House,
　　　　　　　　　　　　　　Marlborough
　　　　　　　　　　　　　　20th June 1915.

Dear Family,

I hope this finds you as it leaves me, with measles? No! I have tried so hard but I can't get it. I believe it is owing to my young, strong and healthy constitution. I will take Christie's wager on and I do pity him having to write all those letters. Mind you write me a long one Christie. The photos are very good though someone has made me look awful gormless in the one of the cameras. The one of the family Levis would be all right if only the apparition on it was taken away. Of course the climbing one is best although you should have waited till I got to the 8th, or was it the 9th step instead of a feeble 5th.

Why you expect me to sweat to Stone Henge I don't know, nasty, cheap. A house scare I call it. I shall go one of these days just to scare you off so none of your lip please. Two people in our house have been made fags. We are quite coming on even with these. I have escaped being turned up, sent over, flogged, swished, caned etc. I broke the back brake of my bone shaker about a month ago and had to pay 2/- to get it mended so I am not rolling (contributions thankfully received). After that I went to Upavon where there is a flying school. We saw about 20 aeroplanes. Some came down while we were there and we saw one about 2 yards off, but it was very dirty. (Weather not aeroplane)!

We did not find a shop until we were nearly home again. We went just 31 miles. While we away an aeroplane came down on the footer grounds. The next day, while we were parading, 4000 of the Black Watch, Gordon Highlanders and some other Scottish Regiments went through. They had marched miles and were very dusty.

A little time ago I had quite an exciting ride of 27 miles. Coming back we had to cross the Downs by a cart track and down one fairly steep hill. My companion was in front when my grid began going faster than I wanted it to, the brakes must have felt tired as they refused to work. Consequently I began to catch him up and had to pass him (a section of the road looks like this: ---u--------u-------). He was in the middle and I passed him on the right hand side getting into the right hand rut, which I could not keep in, so I glided at right angles to the other side of the road with arms and legs anywhere but where they should have been. A kindly thorn bush helped me to get straight – Ow….!!! And I reached the bottom of the hill safely. All at once I heard a snake at my feet and found my back tyre was, well, not absolutely tight. After screaming with laughter for some minutes we decided to mend it. This we did. I was about to get on when I noticed that the air in my front tyre had gone a "long long way to Tipperary" so after a burst of 5 minutes laughter, as we had half an hour to do the last 5 miles of cart track, we mended the front wheel and put the cover back, when suddenly the tyre lever became fed up with working so hard and bit the tyre. So we mended another puncture after a total collapse. We then did speed home, but my companion tried to hurdle a large stone and was let down by his tyre. We mended it and arrived home at about 7.00 (gates at 6.30) but the man (I.W.Taylor) had pity on us so we were not lathered. Two days after we took part in a brigade field day and had to entrench ourselves. We did so and saw some fighting, but at about 8 (this I heard from an officer at the time) the little boys had to get to bed so we refused to retreat and were captured and put under escort by the enemy who seemed about half our number. They had had nothing since breakfast so we gave them what we had left. We then marched back getting to bed about 10 and so got off early school the next day.

A new boy arrived three weeks ago, an American who came over by the Lusitania[1]. He has quite recovered and told us quite a lot of stories. We had another field day the other day. We started at 2.00 and marched about 5 miles, but at about 6.o'clock we heard that the enemy were entrenching themselves so we had to return without doing a thing except wasting an afternoon. Still, on the way back we had a night attack which was great fun as you could see about 2 yards and tripped over everything. We got back about 10.30.

---

1 SS Lusitania was torpedoed by a German U-boat off the Irish coast on 7th May 1915. 1600 died including 128 Americans who had been warned not to sail on her.

A few days after we played the Camerons and were beaten by 18 runs. I am not allowed to bath till the epidemic has stopped, so although the temperature was 82 in the shade a little time ago I can only have a shower and a cold bath. I have been another ride of 35 miles getting back at 7.20 just in time for evening prep.

We consumed 1lb of biscuits and 5 bottles of stuff on the journey as my companion had had no dinner as well as getting one puncture. When we got the tyre off with 2 trouser clips and a pencil, the pencil broke. The Saturday before last I mended three more punctures and cleaned the bike.

There is going to be a camp this year I have heard, between Marlborough, Eton, Charterhouse and that nasty hole Winchester, but it is a private sort of affair and not yet certain. Major Wall, our C.O. has been made a Lieutenant Colonel (Lootenant), the second time this has ever happened to the Commander of a Public School Corps. We got a half-hol and a field day for it, at which we were given a tea. On Friday we played Cheltenham away and won by 9 wickets, some of our people making over a 100.

My poor bike!!! I have taken its 3 speed to pieces and have PUT IT BACK – it runs!!!

Tommy's "balooniplane" SS17 referred to in Vic's letter of 20th June 1917 when Tommy was a 19 year old Sub Lieutenant in the Royal Navy based at Luce near Stranraer.

<u>Willie</u>. I do pity the state of your brain if you can make such a??? !!!

<u>Leonard</u>. Did you use bribery and corruption with the enemies?

<u>Christie</u>. If you don't mind your own business you'll get some licky.

<u>Tommie.</u> Much luck to you and your ballooniplane.

<u>Richie.</u> I'll give you Stonehenge when I get back on the 27th and I'll put licky between the pages of your letter.

<u>Alfie.</u> Help! Murder! Thief! What have I done to offend his Majesty of the Greengages? Don't quote Mr. Anguish.

<u>Irene.</u> Glad to hear you are going strong. Is Tony still strong!! I have changed the tyres of my bike and have bought a puncture proof band.

Tons of love and kisses to all from Vic – The only pebble on the beach!!

To Irene. Has Mrs Colesclough dared to swim with you yet? To Leonard. Have yee no heard of the puir old sqire; he has been vowally murdered.

From Richie. C/o C.S.M. Hawkesworth,
Rugby.
21st June 1915.

Dear cock-sparrows and hen-sparrow.

Glad to see the old F.B. again. It has come round quite quickly this time. Of course, that is due to my order. Everybody seems to be enjoying himself in his own way. I have been doing a fearful sweat this term and am top of the form for the first half term, second in the maths set and have got the best report I ever had. Not bad for a beginner.

I have not done much in the cricketing line, partly because we have spent a lot of time on house matches and Thursday is always a field day. We have only played 2 house matches, but as we have to play two innings, we took 3 half-hols for the first, which we won by an innings and five for the second, which was against the school-house who are cock-house. Neither side has any bowlers. We made 314 and they made about 430. Then we made 409 and got them out for about 230 so we won. The school-house were fearfully sick.

We have had two "Foreigns" (matches against other teams), which we have won. The first against Rugby Town, in which our captain made 210. The other against Clifton was fearfully exciting. They made 399 and we fell to pieces and made 150 so we had to follow on and made about 459, one of our men making 260. So then they went in, and fell to pieces and made 120, their captain making 68. He made 88 in the first innings. One of our men took 2 wickets at the end of one over and 2 in his next.

As some of you may know, I got into the photographical section of the Natural History Society by working so hard in the holidays!!! I have been for one expedition and took 8 photos, but it was very dull so only one has come out, but I had a good tea and held on to a motor a lot of the way. I am becoming rather a good swimmer. I can do a length under water and am entering for the two lengths under 16 (not under water). I have got my study to myself and feel very important using my study companion's bureau. He is ill.

The Corps (a smart body of troops) has been doing a pretty good sweat. It's awful rushing about on very hot days and crawling on your tum-stum-ache with nothing to eat or drink between 2.00 and 7.15. But still, it is good sport. We are much more patriotic than Marlbrs'. We have only a Lt commanding our corps, two captains are serving and various Lt's. Yesterday we had a memorial service for 52 O.R.'s killed since Easter Day. W.H.Raley[1] was one.

They have started a haymaking campaign here. Anyone old enough to do a good days work is going to help the farmers round here, to hoe turnips and toss hay. They are going to wear drill uniform because it is half organised by the War Office. I am too young. We break up on the 28th July. There is going to be a little side camp (i.e. between ourselves) I am not going as there are other things happening at home!! Of course, we shall win the Rugby-Marlborough match!! I heard from Stancliffe the other day, nearly everyone has got measles. Mr Conway has had them. Well, now some sarcastic jaw.

<u>Willie</u>. Don't try and be funny or you will be punished for your puny remarks about cats.

<u>Leonard.</u> You say the fire had to be lighted with paraffin. I suppose it was a paraffin lamp??

<u>Christie.</u> It must be strenuous having a two day operation. What part of the body is it on?? I will take on the wager.

<u>Tommy.</u> I hope the S.S[2]. is ready for use and the best of luck with it, and the worst of luck to the Huns.

<u>Vic.</u> Pretty silly idea shoving pins in your bicycle tyre so as you can have a vulgar guffaw. Don't be rude to my beautiful likeness and machine.

---

1 W.H.Raley was also a friend of the family who lived in Barnsley.
2 An airship. Tommy, at 20 years old, was in command of the SS17 comprising a hydrogen filled gas bag supporting an aeroplane fuselage minus wings and tail plane.

Pom. I shall have to write to your housemaster, Mr Dirty Sweep isn't it, and tell him how rude you are to your revered masters.

Irene. I hope you do some work besides running races and swimming and cleaning ferrets, bants etc.

To all, love from your loving brother,

Richard Elmhirst.

P.S. I hope Willie likes me on my machine.

From Alfred. Chernocke House,
Winchester.
24th June 1915.

Dear Piggy-wigs all.

Welcome back for the old F.B. Well! Quite a lot has happened since I saw this last. I have done a good deal of cricket playing for the 2nd House XI and an under 16 House XI. I wicket keep for them both and have stumped or caught a few people. As I raised a remove last term I have not been very high, 10th out of 19 is my best. I was 16th in the Headmasters exam, but I had to translate just the bit I did not know.[1]

We had the house photo yesterday. I have not seen it yet. Last leave day I went to Farnham and saw "dearest Grandpa". We tried to find a place to have dinner in so we went to a little hole and asked. They said 'yes'. Then we went to a hotel to find out when the buses ran. Grandpa thought, "now this would be a better place to have lunch in", so back we went to the other hole. I have never seen anyone so good at making excuses, it was wonderful. In the end he bought a box of chocolates to console them. Well we did get a jolly good dinner at the hotel.

After dinner we took a bus to a place a good long way away and saw Christie's camp and got a lovely view. By the way Christie, I will take on the ('bet') sorry, 'wager'. I made 15 runs this afternoon and took about 6 wickets bowling. I have passed out in swimming. I had to swim about a hundred yards. We have not won any 'pots' this half. On Tuesday, a leave out day, I am going a bike ride with another man to Southampton and to look round there.

I apologise greatly for having kept this rather a long time, but I have hardly had any time at all. Well, I am going to follow Richie's example with 'sarca remarks'.

---

1 Dad told me that he had learned a large chunk of Vergil by heart in the hope that it would come up for the exam. Unfortunately he got the wrong starting point so his "translation" though perfect in itself bore no resemblance to the chosen text.

Willie: You had better come down here and see me soon or else, the tables will be turned.

Leonard: I believe I am beginning to relax after I saw you. I don't think you had better come down here again. Do you remember the card-sharpers in the train!!![2]

Christie: I have not seen you for years so hurry up before you go out and get 'ki'?!

Tommy: When am I going to see you? I believe the last time I saw you was when you came to Stancliffe and I was in bed and you showed me the snake on your arm.

Vic: What a silly ass you were to go on putting thorns into your tyre till it burst.

Richie: I hope you have got some good photos. I have taken quite a lot but am going to develop them at home. I got 2 envelopes like yours for nothing and you got one for ½ d so I did a good bargain.

Irene: Thank you for your letter which I received on Wednesday. Hurrah, what a lovely idea about Scotland, the motor too. I suppose you have all heard that Daddy sent my bike to me here and I find it very useful too. We are not having so nice weather now as we had a little time ago. A few days ago I saw for the first time two anti-aircraft guns on two motor drays. They did look deadly things. We played a cricket match against one got up by an officer in the 9th Duke er 'Weltons' and I believe Christie's friend was down here to watch, but I wouldn't be certain. We beat them quite easily. I had better stop now as I want to look up some 'mugging'. And I am up to books' in a few minutes.

---

2 Dad told me of the train trip that had a lot of race goers on it. He was inveigled into a session of "spot the queen" by a card sharp, who asked him if he was a sporting man. Dad was allowed to win a couple of rounds before having a large sum taken off him.

Good bye dears, I feel I've got lots more to say, but can't remember it. With love from your loving brother

Alfred Octavius Elmhirst.

Jolly good letter. My longest for the F.B.

From Irene Rachel.

Pindar Oaks,
Barnsley.
28th June 1915.

Dear Family,

Once again, the old F.B. has come my way and very quickly too. We heard on Sunday that Vic has at last got measles. He seems to have wanted them by his letters, anyway he will get them over before the holidays which is something. I will take on Christie's wager, I think it ought to reach him before he goes.

Oaks had his first lesson in leading the other day, (I don't know that you all know that we have called the foal 'Oates') he was funny, he fought more than Pindar did and gave great jumps in the air. He only once got his hooves over the rope. I have got 55 chickens now and we are not going to get any more. I have got a dozen or more R.I.Reds. The bant chicks are now with the big ones, one is a cock and the other a hen. The young cock tried fighting a huge buff hen a little time ago and won.

Dear Grandfather seemed to have a good time on the river. Were the water hens eggs very good; I should think they were all a bit stale. The ladies swimming baths are lovely now we have a water chute though not so long as the one in the new baths. I can just swim four lengths now and Miss Coleclough can swim a width on the water wings and she has only had four lessons.

<u>Willie.</u> If you come home again soon you won't find any little animals on Conus because I washed him this morning so there. I hope you got back before the storm came. We have had a huge storm this morning.

<u>Leonard.</u> I should think the horses and cows frightened you a bit when they called on you in the night up the river. I wonder what the new tent is like. Not as nice as ours. I don't think you seemed to find it a bit stuffy. Your rockery looks fine now and not many hens scratch on it!! And Conus and Tony have not buried many of their biscuits in it!!!

<u>Chris.</u> Tony has not wrecked the tea … again and Conus is quite free from……!! Your photos of Oaks are topping. Mine did not turn out very good. I hope this will reach you before you go. You will have a nice job writing seven letters or else receiving seven letters. Of course, you will have to answer them all so it will come to the same thing!!!

<u>Tommy.</u> I hope you will have your air ship ready soon. Mind you come over and have a look at us in it. I hope the motor bike is going well.

<u>Vic.</u> I hope you aren't very bad, anyway you will get them over before the hols and then to Scotland (when you come back) with the motor. We are going to take a house and take Cook and Emma with us and we can shoot tons of grouse and rabbits and hares and lots of salmon and trout fishing!! And all sorts of things.

<u>Richie.</u> I will give it you when you come home – do I do any work indeed. I hope your bike is going well. I don't expect you have had quite as many punctures as Vic.

<u>Pom.</u> I hope you're getting on all right. You had a good time with Grandpa when he came to see you. You are doing pretty well in the cricket line.

Well Goodbye from your loving sister Irene.

From Tommy.

His Majesty's Air Station
At Walney I, Barrow.
15th July 1915

To the Messrs and Miss Elmhirst.

Dear Everyone,

Many thanks for the F.B. which has come round again and which I have kept for some time as I have been very busy. It will be a fortnight tomorrow since my little ship was completed, but owing to bad weather we have had only three decent flying days and as the new airship station I am going to, Luce Bay near Stranraer, the South West corner of Scotland, not Anglesey, was not quite ready I had to remain here. Unluckily, two days after I had done five trips that day, round about Barrow, our Commanding Officer here went up and smashed the car to pieces when he came down, so I am now without an airship, but am taking the envelope and all the other bits with a new car up to Luce bay to put together there and hope to be flying again in a week's time and shall be able to start patrolling straight away.

18th July 1915

Sheet No 1 was written at Barrow three days ago, but while writing it I was told I had better come up here and see things got ready and then wait for the ship, so here I am. I set off at 2.30 p.m. the other afternoon in pouring rain, but after getting through Kendal and over Shap Fell to Carlisle I had had enough as owing to the rain the belt was slipping and the engine racing so I stopped there for the night, I had to pay 14/- for dinner bed and breakfast and came on here yesterday morning doing the 110 miles in four hours. I did the 180 miles without any breakdown.

It is a very out of the way place here, but the flying ground is perfect which is the main thing. I heard two days ago that I shall (my S.S. being flyable) go out to the Dardanelles with it, most probably in about a fortnight's time. About six of us will most probably go, but the fact is most confidential so don't spread it.

I have been up about a dozen short flights in my airship, and on a decent day it is quite good fun, but always rather a strain on your nerves and while flying you earn every penny of pay you get. However Barrow could not have been a worse place for flying and this could not be much better and if I get out to the Dar.es it should be better still.

As I am responsible for C not getting the F.B. this round (at least I believe I am) you had better all write to me and complain about it. I went down to Anglesey the other day and had a good look round there, so I have been getting about a bit lately. I have got a few SS[1] photos, but will leave them at home if I go out so you can see them there.

If you come up Scotland way before I shove off, you had all better look in here. There is not much to see however and you would have to stop the night at the pub I am putting up at.

Much love to all from

Your ever affect, Brother T.W.E

---

1   His airship (see photo on page 69).

(TO AUNTY MIN)
From Christie.

8th D. of WS
32nd Bde.
11th Div.
Br. Medit. Exp. Force.
Thursday.
July 15th 1915.

Dear Auntie Min,

I believe I have a letter of yours to answer, so here goes. I censor my own letters & as I am put on my honour as regards letting out information I cannot say everything I should like to. I am writing this in a little tent I purchased in England (wt. 2 1/2 lbs) & it is a perfect joy. The C.O. is the only other person with a tent. We live in as few clothes as possible under a boiling sun from 5.30 am. to 6.30 pm. & we bathe twice a day; the sea is warm and one can stay in for hours without getting cold.

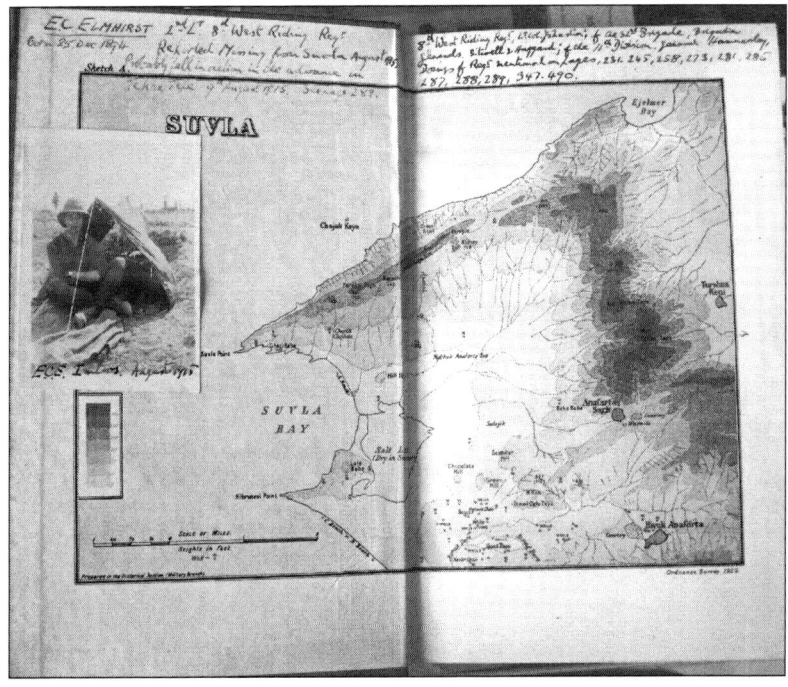

Inside cover of a book about the Gallipoli campaign with notes on Christie plus a photo of his tent.

We are on a very large island about 60 miles from the Dardanelles & our Regiment is bivouacked about 50 yds from a large bay in which we bathe. The troops have not been long on the island, the supplies are nothing grand & our menu is nearly always the same. Breakfast, bacon, bread (or biscuit) tea (no milk) & when I can get eggs. Lunch, bully beef, cucumber & melon & tea. For tea, tea, bread & jam, and "Dinner", bully beef, cucumber, melon and tea. We brought a few provisions off the ship, but they do not go far; Greek hawkers come round and have set up a kind of bazaar & try to get extortionate prices from everyone and often succeed. The only thing to do is to put down half the price they ask and take the goods. They shout a bit, but they know they have got a good thing out of you. One can often get 22/- or 23/- in change for a gold sovereign[1] although I haven't done that yet, but they try to make you pay 6d for a melon, 8 eggs 1/- and cucumbers 3d.

They understand no English except "lemonade" which they sell in jugs @ 3d. so it is rather hard making them understand; they speak Greek. We had a ripping, but very thrilling trip on the Acquitainia & on the Sunday after we set sail we were missed by 12 yards. That was not the only sub episode, but you may get more news later. We wait patiently for news from home. Where we are now no news whatever reaches us, only rumours from the Dardanelles. I would say a lot more about goings on here if I could. Nine out of my platoon are down with a touch of the sun.

Saturday. Several things have happened. I am very sick about one thing & that is that I go to Base Depot with the Res M.G.[2] Section & wait there until casualties occur. Isn't it sickening. I went to a Greek village on Friday and made a purchase or two from the stores. It was a very funny little village. Yesterday we had an inspection by some General. I am glad to say it didn't last above an hour. The Mauretania has arrived here with some troops. I am trying to get on her in order to get provisions.

---

1 Britain did not abandon the gold standard until 1919 so a gold sovereign (20 shillings) was still legal tender although paper £1 notes and 10/- notes were being issued in 1914.

2 M.G = Machine Gun.

What my men want more than anything else in the world are "Wild Woodbines" I think France gets the majority that are collected so our poor fellows go without. If you know of anyone collecting such things you'll be able to give them the tip.

I hope all at home (i.e. round the neighbourhood) are well. If they keep as fit as I am doing they'll be all right. Any books, magazines, newspapers are always welcome. We've had no mail for a fortnight now. Well, Goodbye till the next time of writing from your affectionate nephew and Godson, E. Chris. Elmhirst.

A scrapbook from August 1915 showing Christie, his tent and a photo of the fighting men Tommy, Willie and Christie. Also the newspaper cuttings reporting his death.

From Alfred.

Pindar Oaks,
Barnsley.
July 38th [sic] 1915.

Dear Christie,

It would be unsportsmanlike to forget that wager which you won so I am doing so now. We had Aunty Min's cricket match yesterday. I made 81 not out and bowled 2 people. I hope you are not quite expiring from lack of everything out there. I wonder what the films are like, I haven't seen them yet. How bad of you to ask for some more.

I go back to Winchester on the 15th September. Daddy, Uncle Harry and Vic went to Coumes for bees today, but the motor broke down so they didn't get back till late. Leonard is quite good at riding Tommy's motor bike. Richie and I had tea at the Rookery this afternoon, we had games afterwards. I believe we are taking my and Richie's bikes to Scotland. Both Conus and Tony are going with us to Scotland. We are trying to rid Tony of his hoppers, which is going to be a hard job.

It's been raining hard today. I expect that's what you'd like most. This pen is awful, but I hope you will be able to read this. I am getting angry with it. Irene, Richie and I went fishing yesterday at Ouslethwaite. Richie caught a 1lb perch. A good many of the others were pretty big too.

Mind you get slightly wounded and come home and get a good long leave, but whatever you do, don't get 'nipped by a fast one' or – well I shall be sixth in the family then. One of your letters came here in ten days, which is pretty good isn't it. Leonard is keeping F.B. quiet till we get back to our respective schools. I suppose you will want a motor-bike if you ever come back. I'm rather good at riding one, it's quite easy.

Well, there is no more news now, so love to you and your skin from your loving brother

Alfred.O.Elmhirst

In Memory of

Second Lieutenant Ernest Christopher Elmhirst

*8th Bn., Duke of Wellington's (West Riding Regt.)
who died aged 20 on Saturday, 7th August 1915.*

Second Lieutenant Elmhirst, Son of the Rev. W. H. and Mrs. Elmhirst, of "Elmhirst," Barnsley.

*Remembered with honour
HELLES MEMORIAL, Turkey.*

*In the perpetual care of
the Commonwealth War Graves Commission*

Christie's "In Memoriam" Information.

From Leonard   P&O.S.S.Co
                                S.S
                                Sept 1915

The sea is rough but

I have my sea legs.

My dear Grandchildren,

I have <u>at last</u> come to the conclusion that F.B. Esq shall start once more on his journeys, & I intend to book his passage when I get to Port Said which should be within a few days. His procedure will I'm afraid be sadly out of order. I cannot send to C[1] because he does not know his address, perhaps you do by this time. I hope so. I had meant making enquiries at the hospital at Malta but we passed the island without calling at 3.0 this morning.

I am in the unhappy position of not having had news from home for two weeks, & of being without chance of hearing anything for another 3 weeks at least, then I shall expect a whole mail bag. Don't be afraid of writing, twice a week if you can catch the Indian mail, & "it's a long way", etc.

Now for the latest stop press news. As you know I left our mountain resort with many regrets. Still of an evening, as I sit down to a 6 or 7 course dinner (at 6.30 however, & I don't have any tea) I hear such strains as

"There flew a duck at 60 ft (yards) high
And Daddy shot it quite close by
And we all wiped our eyes (with surprise, oh no!) and cried
Not for us, not for us"
With any suitable accompaniment such as Uncle C. & his port wine!

---

[1] This seems to suggest that Leonard was not yet aware of Christie's death although he makes no reference to Christie in the personal notes at the end of his letter.

Or

"The Moor is now of grice bereft

Because of Leonard's* right and left

*Editor's comment, 'The name of an extinct animal related to the Dodo, from the Archipelago.

And we all clapped our hands & cried

Was it grice?

Other things also come flitting into my brain. Now for some of us Le grice, ah yay were too rapeed, but of ye hares (especially Tommy's) & ye mountain savages, oh well.

As I lay in my bunk, in the Bay of Biscay (poitry) certain phrases kept running in my head as my breakfast ran (crossed out) oh no, shame! – such as the beard of a goat, the punch of a ram, the bones of a sheep – I can't remember any others but in the midst of the night, ghosts would scamper about my cabin, armed with fowling pieces, & gibber & moan in the bushes.

I have been looking at the past letters of the F.B. I see references to "lots of salmon fishing". I have no recollection of this matter. At the moment, we are in the submarine danger zone, so you may never get this letter.

Well, I had an excellent tea with "the McDixon" & not a bad journey down to town (Mother will correct me here) & quite a pleasant time in town, spent first with Mr Gamage [?] at his residence in Holborn then with Lord Kitchener at his cottage in Whitehall & then Mrs Fry in the Mansion close to Hyde Park. I also visited the Psalmist whom some of you know, his wound is almost recovered.

Then onto the ship, I knew I should be ill, I had felt it in the motor, & the train, & I realised my feelings as we went down the channel. Only twice however and I was never too dazed to read. I was however glad when we left the bay. Life is quite interesting on board. I sleep in a cabin for 2. The 2nd passenger is a small boy who is hauled out of bed at 7.0 every morning by his mama, who I am glad to say has now ceased to polish him up in my cabin and takes him to her own. Consequently in the day time I have it to myself, with water laid on, & an electric fan, a great joy and most necessary. It runs all night and since I have no porthole life would be unbearable without it. 7.0 I am called by a steward who used to bring tea & biscuits and fruit, i.e. green apples, which can be chewed but not swallowed.

7.30 or later I arise, don my Gibraltar dressing gown & assail the bathroom where I take a cold & boring tub, <u>never a hot one</u>. Breakfast 8.30 with a good choice of dishes suitable to my highly developed palate. Breakfast to lunch writing, reading or chess. I'm ready to take anyone on at chess & get beaten. After lunch perhaps a doze or a stroll on deck which is fairly crowded, then more chess or reading in the evening. At Gib. We had 6 hours, 4 of us took a carriage & some lovely white grapes & careered round the town & very nearly all round the rock, they are making a road right round it. The rock itself is a ramshackle affair, & looks as though it would crumble to pieces in no time. The people are interesting but terrible scamps, ready to do you at any moment. By walking out of a shop twice my friend, a 1st class bargainer, brought down my dressing gown from 30/- to 13/-. I would have given up the attempt long before.

It was the same in Marseilles, everyone out to have on the wretched foreigner, especially the guileless Englishman. So far I consider I have come thro very well. At Marseilles I went to see the Indian soldiers camp, most interesting. You can also get 2 glasses of wine for 30 ctmos. i.e. pence. But it stinks like nothing on earth & is altogether an unpleasant city.

Sometimes we are visited by flocks of birds which are very tame and hop about on the deck chairs. Tomorrow we hope to be at Port Said where I shall post this letter. At Aden I change ships & go on to Bombay. Then I shall be frizzled up.

To Willie. When are they going to make you a captain. Tommy I hope you have had some good shooting after getting your eye in on hares. Vic I hope you will goats beard Stonehenge this term and bring the iron shins into play. Richie I hope you caught your friend in the burn before you left. Pom I haven't a notion have you. Irene write & tell me all about the journey home & your friend Johnson. I can still hear a whisper in my Mist Lennard – Gipsies.

Much love to all, Leonard

From Willie.   Parkridge Bank Camp,
                                Stafford.
                                Oct. 13th 1915.

Dear Family,

Here's our old friend turning up again, four months since be visited me last. He didn't want to spend long with me but I've persuaded him to stop a fortnight. I've seen nearly everybody since he came to me last so I needn't say much. You see I've changed my address again. I think I've had a different one each time I've written so far. The Battalion or what's left of it is probably here for the winter, whether I shall be or not, I don't know. I may go out, I may stop here as Company Commander or I may go as an instructor to the new Machine Gun Corps that is now being formed. You may have heard that I've got my third star & am now a Captain.

This week I'm extra busy as my boss the Brigade M.G. Officer has been sick & has now gone off on sick leave, so I'm doing his job & have to make arrangements for M.G. sections of three Battalions to come back here on Saturday from Newcastle under Lyme, & for the landladies of their billets to be paid, & for my section to go over there for next week to shoot, & several other things. I'm hoping to get home for a day or two after next week as I shall then have another twenty machine gunners ready for the front. We had half a dozen generals round inspecting this morning, Lieut. Gen. Sir Bruce Hamilton, Maj. Gen. Lawson, Maj Gen. Campbell & three Brigadiers, a fine collection of redhats. I got orders to have some people firing on the range here in case Bruce Hamilton wanted to hear one of our guns popping. However he hadn't time. Very hard lines on him missing an introduction to a nice chap like me. Why, my grateful country thinks I'm worth £230 a year to her now & gives me another £55 for putting me into a hut with no furniture in it! I expect a horse turning up for me in a few days. Its saddle & bridle arrived a week ago. I've done quite a lot of riding lately as our second in command lends me his nag almost whenever I want it.

You may have heard something about correspondence in the Army. You see letters in Punch sometimes imitating it. I've just come across a fine example of it in our Battalion. The correspondence has reached twelve sheets of foolscap paper now, & is still going on. It's been to York & Leicester & one or two other places & it's all about the number of a voucher for four bars of soap which were bought & paid for some three months ago!

<u>Leonard</u> Glad to hear you've found a warmer climate than this. Your query as to my shove is answered.

<u>Tommy</u> I hear you've been making good practice with & at dummies. Why not have a go at the real thing. You might write a longer Reference Sheet next time. I think I had better begin to economize & write on O.H.M.S. paper or on Memo forms.

<u>Vic</u> What is the matter with your beard? I think you & your bike ought to go on the stage & do two breakdowns & lightning repairs with trouser clips etc. a night.

<u>Richie</u> Now I know how it was my bike went wrong last summer. I suspected it.

<u>Pom</u> I don't like the name you give the rest of the family. I hope you are working hard & have made some nice friends! Are you top of the school this term & do you put your bedsocks on each night & brush your dirty little teeth before you lie down in your little sty?

<u>Irene</u> I've just written to you. Mind you write back. You might wash Conus once a week to celebrate my effort.

Much love to you all from your affect.te brother

Willie.

From Vic.   Preshute House,
                                    Marlborough.
                                    23rd Oct 1915.

Dear Family.

I hope you are all having a fairly good time this term. I have lasted through half the term and am feeling very satisfied with myself. We have begun to get cold weather now and I have to keep all my clothes on my bed at night to get warm. Yesterday we stopped having early school at 7 o'clock as it is changed to 7.25. The extra 25 minutes make an enormous difference, but I still get up so late that there is hardly any time to wash. Of course, I wash whether it makes me late or not.

We are having an extra amount of Corps work this term. I suppose it is meant to teach us a lot, but it is quite often a farce. Last Saturday we had night operations for those who go to the classes of instruction. We started out at 7 o'clock and landed back frozen at about 11.00. As the company on our right went a mile too far forward we lost touch with it so it was not much good. Consequently, when we got back, we were told that we needed a lot more practice and should get it!!!

We started rugger about a fortnight ago and, though the ground has been hard, we have been having some excellent games. At the beginning of the term we were supposed to be the worst House and would be bottom in House matches. We have had two of these and drew the first, 8 points each, and won the second, 32-nil so may be able to get into Cock House match. I still play full back and managed to get my House Upper last match. We had a really good field day a little time ago. We started out at 9 am and got back at 6pm. We marched about two miles and then went onto the downs. I was in the Rear Guard of the Russian Army and we were retreating slowly before the Germans. We had to keep them from crossing a river before a certain time and we did so, though just at the end our platoon was outflanked by the enemy and in getting back we ran straight into an enemas'[sic] platoon before they knew we were there. There were no casualties though it nearly ended in a burn.

I have to write a week end prep now. This time it is a précis, but it will not take very long. I have been reading a very exciting book just now, but have finished it and so have time to write this!! I had a very good time last Sunday. Tons of cash, a box of toffee and a cake. All very good. There is a tame jackdaw here and on Sundays it comes into the Hall and has a really good feed. The first time it caused a great sensation as it caws hard or tries to, it really makes a sort of squeak. I have just been down to the town to brew as this and Tuesday afternoon are the only times I get. I spent ninepence and had an ice, an egg, some bread and butter and lemonade. I should have thought they would have stopped having ices now as it is colder, but they are very good, especially after a long perspiration!!

I do not seem to have as much to write about as some of these people seem to have written. If you want to know how I am getting on in work, I shan't tell you ("so there", as Irene would say) because I do not know; as now I am one of the knuts!! I do not get weekly orders. Ere I stop, which will be f-air. Tuesday I may know my half term orders. I must be c-air-ful not to go down although I feel weary and t-ire-d as that would be so t-yre-some and you would cair-some (I wager you). I have been writing now the whole afternoon and the air is getting used up so I will prep-air to open the window. Th-eir, I have finished a few of them. I leave the rest for Richie and Alfie to enlarge upon.

Willie. Many congratulations on your promotion. I hope it is worthy of you. Anyhow you seem to be doing a little work now. I suppose we look forward (a long way) to seeing you a Major. What's that about a beard, I know I only singe mine as yet, but it is certainly not longer than ½ an inch, or perhaps you wish to present me with a razor. More bike talk, how's tiresome; mine is now at home, of course the tyre is a big puncture stuck together with an outfit, but I think it grows holes when not in use.

My Uncle in India. You know the one who came home inside a (not in cider) tiger. You forgot the octopus grapple, rabbit squeak etc.

You ought to write to Gladys about the ghosts and see if she has recovered from her Lassintullichrichnen. Will you try if stones roll down Mt Everest like they do down Schiehallion? You are mistaken about the "Salmon fishing", there was heaps of it though perhaps the salmon were a bit scarce. Did you have the family Shetland oilskin on while you were in the Bay of Biscay feeding the submarines? Did the little boy in your cabin ever refuse to be washed with….?!! My iron pins have no chance this term as it is not hockey, also Stonehenge is too far away. As Alfie is going to tell you about the return journey I will only perhaps put in a page or two from my diary.

Tommy. Can we now spread the confidential fact that you are going to the Dardanelles? Have you had any more surprise calls yet? Daddy and I had a hare drive before we left but I don't think we got so many as you did.

Vic. Best wishes and I am glad you are doing so remarkably well.

Richie. You think a jolly sight to mach your self. All our Lt's who could go have gone and the rest are not allowed to go as they have to teach us because (firstly) we learn everything so quickly and well we need a good many people to teach us and (secondly) the War Office, seeing how good we are, let us have good officers who know something about the business. I now have 10 hours a day work on three days a week, can you beat that (not including meal times). I really must retire from the discussions on my bike.

Uncle Octy. You really are a thorn in my side. You make me perspire. I quite agree with you in saying that your letter is long, a lot too long I think. You will have a nice lot to write about but remember the …… grouse. Have you sent your bill in? If not you will have to receipt yourself. (Do you remember?)

Aunt Rachel. I won't mention those nasty home truths about Tony and Conus. I hear from your letter here that I have got measles. I hope it is not true. There, I hope to see this nair mair for a long time. I have given over making puns. There is an owl here which is worse than the young one at Lass[1]; it does not howl but screeches every night.

At last I have finished. Much love from all to Vic, also the other way round from Vic.

---

1 Lassintullich.

From Richie.   C/o C.S.M.Hawkesworth,
                                Rugby
                                2nd November 1915

Dear Peoples, Nations, Languages etc,

I'm glad to see Old Mr Frank Budget, he is frank about what he says. This is the first time I have kept him more than two days. It seems that Willie is getting a bad name. Every time F.B. comes to him he has changed his address and now he says he's got three stars. I suppose he means three stripes!!!

I am having quite a decent term. I have come out 5th for the half term and have got a fairly decent report, not bad for first term in the form. I am also a "bloomin' buddin' bugler'" and I ought to be in the band at the end of term. On Tuesday we are going to have a decent field day with Eton at a place in Bucks. I have got a study to myself this term as my study companion has not come back yet. We started late hours this morning; we get up at 7am. Yesterday was Founders Day, we only had one lesson. We had a service at 12 with a sermon about missions in India. On Sunday we had a topping lantern lecture about a mission in Kashmir. A little time ago we had a frightfully dry lecture on the strategic geography of the War.

We are doing musketry this term instead of gym because there are not enough gym instructors. I have not done much in the footer line this term. I have been captain of a side twice, the second time we only lost by one try. On Saturday we play Cheltenham, we have got two people in the XV.

I see that Pom has to write about our journey home[1]. I hope he puts more than what Vic calls his diary. Anyway, Johnson got us home in less time than Eyre took, with only one burst tyre. I think Leonard will have got my letter now telling about half the journey, it might be put in F.B. The headmaster is going the round of the forms. He came to ours three times and took a Latin class himself, which we did not know at all, but we were very intelligent in an English lesson later.

---

1   The journey from the shooting holiday at Lassintullich near Loch Rannoch and Loch Tummel.

<u>Willie.</u> Sir Bruce Hamilton was pretty lucky not having enough time to see you. It seems there is always somebody who is ill for you to take their place. It is so nice for you.

Daddy long legs, or Grandad, or Dodo. I hope you have received my note about the journey. You ask about the salmon fishing. There was plenty of it. I caught a salmon and saw the big one three times. I wonder if you heard anything about "rennet and figs" instead of 7 course dinners which are not for me. You say you are a stink animal I see?!! ………..and now…..w he's gone….e aloft.

<u>Tommy.</u> I hear you are going to take Willie for a ride. You will be able to fill your small reference sheet with his fears or exclamations of joy.

<u>Vic.</u> You give yourself and say too many airs. Mind you don't Tummel into the habit of it. What is the joke about the goats beard, or is it your beard. We have now in the Corps, two captains, two Lts and 1 2nd Lt and we are a jolly smart lot.

<u>Alfie.</u> I hear you have been doing some registration work lately and you made a mess of it? You will have to write a lot about the journey, especially "grice" which was very much up aloft.

<u>Irene.</u> How is your lickey cat, I have got your black one on my shelf.

Hoping that the Budget may be bulging more than ever when he comes to me next time.

Much love to all from

Richie.

From Alfred.

Chernocke House,
Winchester.
8th Nov 1915.

Dear Sirs and Siress.

I hope you are all quite well, as I am not. I have got rather a bad cough, a cold and a few other things. Well whether well or ill, no matter, the long-lived F.B. puts that all right when it comes. I join the Corps next half, and have been there a year then, and a jolly fine place it is too.

In our Corps, we have a 'Major', a 'Captain', a 'Lieutenant' and three '2nd Lieutenants'. Oh! Do you say I have to write about the journey home, I forget how that came to pass, please some one tell me. Well, I suppose I had better do it or else there will be a row with everybody[1].

We at last got off. No we didn't, a lot happened before that. We were to start at 7.oclock am punct. That doesn't mean puncture. I shall never finish at this rate shall I! At 7am Johnson Esq found out he hadn't got an accumulator, so off we had to go to Kinloch Rannoch to get it. Great excitement when he came back, the luggage was tied on at last, Conus in, and his basket. Goodbyes to Campbell and John and Sweep. Great cheers as we start off in great style. Aberfeldy was reached at last, after going at 47 mph once. We sent the game hamper off there, which was a great relief as it took up most of the room. Crieff was the next fairly big town I believe. I know there will be many disagreements over this. We lost our way just before we had lunch and had to go down cart-tracks and narrow paths before we got right.

A platoon of wasps raided us while lunching, but we bravely sustained the attack of the enemy without casualties. We went through Glasgow without losing ourselves and began to near Carlisle when we came to two

---

1 Papa Elmhirst had rented a grouse moor at Lassintullich (including Schiehallion) and fishing rights on the river Tummel. He hired a saloon coach for the family which was hitched on to various trains (including by tradition, the Flying Scotsman). Leonard, Vic, Richie and Pom were driven up by George Eyre (The Barnsley motor dealer) so he could teach the groom J.J.Johnson how to drive. Johnson drove back unaided even though he had not yet mastered reverse.

notices and two roads to Carlisle. We were wondering which we should go by when the 'airy' man saw a notice; 'road up' bridge being mended or something like that so we had to go miles round to get to Carlisle. We got petrol here. Just outside the town, when, as it was practically pitch dark, we thought we had better find a place to camp out in, we enquired at two places and at last found one, so we got 'the motor' into the yard and unpacked. Johnson slept in the car and we were taken out to a field and pitched one tent (not Leonard's). We were visited in the middle of the night by a cow, who wished to pay his call. We did not sleep very well, but enjoyed ourselves very much. We had an excellent home-cooked breakfast, but the 'Primus' wanted its master, so it wouldn't act very well for us. Well, again we set off and went through some lovely country round the Lake District. Now comes the 'tasty part'!!! We bought four bottles of ginger beer somewhere near Kendal and we went some way out of town, when we thought we had better have lunch so we stopped, gave Johnson his eatables and had some sandwiches ourselves. And then what we most looked forward to, got out a 'grice'. Oh, it did look so good, we took a knife and cut a slice out of the breast,

"Vic put in a knife

And pulled out a slice,

But what should he find there

But 'lice' inside grice!!!"

Don't you think that is jolly well put? Greedy Vic ate nearly everything except this. Well, we put 'Him' in the tool-box for Conus, how he did enjoy it. When we were within talk of home, what should happen, but "Bang"!! The poor front tyre had been tired of life so gave it up, but he'd done his duty. We had to fill up with petrol and oil a few more times and at last we reached Wakefield. Oh, to think he had landed us within ten miles of home. But what was more, he did get us home by 4.10 pm that afternoon.

We had tea and went to see the 'rooks', who were quite surprised. Daddy, mother, Irene, A.F. and Tony would arrive sometime, so we went to the station in case they came. Wonders! They did! But we met them in style having come home with an average of 25 m.p.h. So ended the most delightful holiday with the mountains and lochs of Scotland.

Willie: I can't stand all this cheek from a 'bloomin Cap'n'. You wait. 'I'll larn yer' if you're not off.

Leonard: Well Grandpa, and how's everything going with you? I hope you don't mind me taking one of those stamps on your letter for my collection. I still have a scent in my nose 'Mist Alfie Grice'!!!

Tommy: Do come down here in the Airship. Glad about the new engine, hope all goes well.

Vic: You really are a disgrace to the family. We are still getting up at 6.30am and get to bed at 9pm. I was 'continent' that is in sick room yesterday, but am 'abroad' i.e. well again today. Glad the footer is going well.

Richie: You are swanks at Rugby and you think a lot too much of yourselves.

Irene: Love to Tonus and Cony and everything. How are the horses? I think Conus almost deserves a wash for Willie's little effort.

Well, goodbye all my dears.

Love from your loving brother Alfred Elmhirst.

From Irene Rachel.   Pindar Oaks Hall,
                                      Barnsley
                                      29th November 1915.

Dear Family,

I hope you are all in the best of health. I have kept F.B. rather a long time, but then I am so busy!! Willie will say that's a fib of course. I am well up in live-stock and all are going along very well. Not many of you have seen the ferrets except Willie and Tommy. They are very lively (themselves I mean). Somebody will say that something else on them is lively I expect, but they at least are free. Just lately they have been having a fine feast (it's a good job that nobody reads this who loves cats or kittens). One of Uncle Bert's cats has had kittens and as he has tons of cats already and does not want any more, he asked me if I should like the kittens for the ferrets; at the time I did not know that ferrets liked kittens, but now I do. They like them better than any rabbit or rat and you should have seen them fighting.

Uncle Bert came to tea yesterday and said there were two more waiting when those were disposed of. I went up to fetch them in the afternoon!!! Conus is very well and is very interested in the ferrets and, as they (they ferrets) now have an open air run, he and Tony can sit and watch them. Conus, if I am not looking, tries to catch them through the wire and runs round and round and gets very excited, but he gets a smack when I catch him doing that – bad dog. I washed him in one of the tin baths on Friday. He was very dirty, but nothing else; he then, next day, got his paws rather dirty so had to be dipped in again, which was not quite to his taste as he had to be chased round the house and in the house before I cotched him, just because he saw me with a towel and my sleeves rolled up.

He has just learned a new trick "to wave his paws", and he does it topping now. It is the best trick of the season. Miss Coleclough says he does it too fast, but he only does it fast when he is hungry and, nearly always when he has had a good meal, he won't hardly do it at all except if you have a piece of sugar or something nice that suits 'His Majesty's taste'!!

Tony lives in the stable now as he got the "rumatis" in his kennel at the back door and could hardly walk sometimes. Now he is quite alright and does not lumber along, but trots quite sedately and, when in a good mood, condecends to run a little. We take him with us on our walks now though Miss Coleclough said we should have to give him up because he would lag and I had to stay behind a little to half drag and half haul wretched Tony along. But now, as his "rumatis" is better and he is not so fat, now he goes quite all right. Conus of course runs miles ahead and gets up fights with every dog he meets if he can and then we have to extract him with Tony's help. One day he went for a huge retriever dog and began by nipping his hind legs (he always begins like that) then runs away, but this dog would not be played with and turned around on Conus and nabbed him very neatly in the neck as he was about to run away. He put him on the ground on his back and got him by the throat. We thought this time he would get it hot and ran to the rescue, so did the man who the dog belonged to. Conus got up, his dignity rather ruffled, but not a bit hurt and wanted to go at the dog again, but we held him. The man said that we ought to have chosen better sides. I suppose he thought we had set Conus onto his dog.

We thought we might have got some skating this week as it has been freezing all day since Friday and the ice today was quite two inches thick if not more. We stood on the edge and pushed Conus out and he slipped about, but did not like it very much, but this evening it began raining and so does not look very hopeful. We had got out the skates too and got them ready. Spider is very well, so is Doctor. The foals are very lively and Pindar looks lovely. Oaks is very shaggy and rather dejected. The bants are in very good health and can fly better than ever. They have not begun laying yet. I often go shooting now on Saturday with Daddy and Uncle Bert, we have great fun.

<u>Willie.</u> If you put in the F.B. what you said when you were here you will catch it so mind what you say. Conus is very well and I washed him the other day and the water was very dirty, but nothing was floating in it.

<u>Grandpa.</u> I hope you are getting on alright. I shall not soon forget Uncle Charles and his port wine!! We could hear him in the drawing room I remember.

Tommy. Have you got your engine trouble right yet, praps you will be coming down soon for a little longer leave next time. Conus was very dejected the evening you went off.

Vic. I should think praps you will have learned better manners when you come home talking about "those nasty little home truths". What about not being able to get to Stonehenge, such an easy ride, but then what could we expect from such a little boy as you. All the puns are very poor, not even as good as the Tummel ones.

Richie. Mind you have learned to blow the bugle when you come home then you can give us lessons.

Pom. You ought to have weighed the F.B. before you sent it off as Daddy had to pay 2d more on it so we shall have to write on thin paper.

Well, I must finish up now as Mother and Miss C. are both pining to get me off to bed and are saying they are sure I have written long enough!!!!

With love from your loving sister

Irene.

Miss Coleclough (Irene Rachel's Governess) with Tony the family spaniel.

From Tommy.

Naval Airship Station,
Luce Bay,
Stranraer.
3rd December 1915.

Dear Family,

The F.B. has come round again after a prolonged absence, but it is all the more welcome, though I am afraid after its trip to India my news will be rather stale however I think every one will agree that the chief object of the F.B. is to provide a good amount of news to the one who is away from England. I still remain at Luce Bay but I expect the next round will find me away, either near Chatham or somewhere on the East Coast. This last weekend I have had Willie up here, but most unfortunately he was not able to have a trip in my airship as we had a gale of wind blowing the whole three days he was here and no flying was possible, however he filled up his time all right with some hockey, billards, looking for stone age relics, and helping to stalk wild ducks with a Lewis machine gun, we did not get anything that day, but two days before got a wild goose and four wild duck with it.

I tried to get a few days at home ten days ago but was recalled back to work the afternoon I got home and so spent 30 hours travelling for nine hours at home, however I did a lot in the day and not having leave then may get a few days about Christmas time. I have been doing a good deal of flying but have only had one excitement, when I broke down about halfway across the channel and after drifting about and dropping in the water twice, managed by throwing every moveable thing we had on board overboard to clear the cliffs and land among a herd of cows in a grass field in County Antrim, Ireland. I had quite a good time there and came back the next day after packing everything in.

I have sold my motorbike and got as much as I gave for it which was not bad, but it was really in better condition than when I bought it as the Insurance Company paid for new front forks, front wheel, new tyres, new lamp, new tool bag, new handle bars, and both new mudguards on account of the various smashes I had. I have now got another one, a

Douglas, but the roads and weather are so bad here that I am thinking of selling it again before I break it up too.

Well I think I have finished scraping all the news I can remember since I last saw the remaining authors of the budget so I will answer a few questions.

<u>W.</u> With reference to your reference to my short reference sheet, this paper having run out, my only way of referring to the F.B. was on a reference sheet.

<u>L.</u> If this reaches you in time for Christmas it brings all good wishes also a photo of myself, for you if you want it.

<u>V.</u> Glad to hear you got your House Upper, but I should advise getting into hen houses, you have had practice at them.

<u>R.</u> With reference to your reference re. my reference sheet I refer you to my reference W.

<u>A.</u> I am afraid <u>Winchester</u> is rather a long way to come in the airship.

<u>I.</u> I am glad to say my engine troubles have subsided but I expect by the time this reaches you it will have had many more as it much prefers to be ill, than keep well.

I hope this finds you all as it leaves me with all good wishes for the New Year from

Tommy.

From Leonard.
                          Army Y.M.C.A.
                          Ahmeduagan,
                          Deccan,
                          India
                          Jan.1.1916.
          (Notice I have got it right the 1st time)

Dear Family,

I hardly know where to begin, unless I start off by saying that the F.B. was never more welcome. It arrived on the Tuesday after Christmas to find me laid up with "funicula tonsillitis", not "change of food" though I don't say that Christmas fare had nothing to do with it, for I did have my share. However that's a thing of the past now & I am almost in the land of the living again. Christmas eve we balled through most of the old friends at a service in church, I'd rather have been doing it outside Mr Banham's, do you remember?

Still, afterwards I came back & prepared for a dinner for 10 soldiers here, they ate until they couldn't eat any more, Pindar Oaks mince pies, duck, lamb(!) cutlets plum pudding soup crackers fish coffee cigars lemonade chocolates & oranges. This is not the exact order but by the end I want you to think of them all mixed up inside, then onto my verandah where we kept the game up until 12.0. Christmas day I didn't eat anything until 1.0 lunch which I had with an Indian & his wife in their fashion.

I had some more somewhere else then an enormous spread with one of the American Missionaries, I did my best not to eat too much then I was driven home 5.0, & lay down in order to prepare for dinner that night with the Colonel, his wife & the Adjutant. I did not want it. However as you see, it was a stirring Christmas. The soldiers were looked after by the Regiment. By 5pm 90% were dead drunk & by 10pm most of the officers & sergeants were as bad & then the Indian gets up & says, "if this is how you Christians celebrate the birth of your founder, I'm not having any".

I've not seen a snake alive yet, a cobra shot between my feet one night when I was lighting my cycle lamp but I had no leisure to examine it.

My gardener servant & boy are having good games outside, they are paid at the rate of 8 – 10/- a month & they think it their duty to show the inhabitants of the place the sort of master they have. This they do by spending all their savings & perhaps pawning their wives last evening dress in order to buy a new turban & a more brilliant striped shirt each.

The gardener is only a boy his work is done on this wise. Imagine yourself going into the garden at Pindar Oaks & finding a bed of 1st class rose trees newly planted, the gardener tells you he has them from a friend, two days later you walk into your greenhouse & see that half of your newly rooted carnation cuttings have gone, you may protest but it is a little use.

Luckily in my compound there is little worth taking so I gain & day by day without paying extra I see new beds being planted & new cuttings arriving. Now & then I am presented with a beautiful buttonhole, but I know that the rose tree only grows in Mrs So & So's garden. However its no use making a fuss, all the gardeners belong to one caste or class & on the whole you stand to gain rather than lose by keeping quiet, besides I only understand 2 words of his lingo.

My washerman lives on the premises, but he washes for so many other people that I don't pay him anything! He uses my water. So things go on in this country. The Englishman is regarded by the servant as a kind of God especially if he's a big Sahib i.e. a gentleman, & this they soon spot.

I paid a visit to Lucknow in November & went over all the mutiny ground, much of which has been untouched since then. Then I had a few days at Delhi where I learnt to smoke an Indian hookah, (you hand it round, just giving the mouthpiece a wipe before sending it on to the next man) & explored the ground which is being prepared for the new capital. Imagine an undulating plain covered as far as you can see (& a bit further) with ruins of old cities, palaces & forts. The Delhi itself is a fascinating place also Agra & the Taj Mahal, one of the wonders of the world, & truly so.

I enclose a few photos, with instructions.

Captain Yes the climate at the moment could not be pleasanter, cool at nights, pleasant breezes & sunshine by day, but wait a month or so. I see you will be in a position to finance the family on your return.

Tommy Thank you very much for an excellent photo of yourself & your hobby horse, it reminds me of a cigar, & by the way for my Xmas dinner 50 cigars cost the same as a box of 12 crackers in England, i.e. 2/- I hope the motor bike found a good owner it was a pleasant machine especially when there was a bump in the road.

Vic – In case the iron shins get rusty try a little coarse sandpaper or emery cloth "Tons of cash" sounds good, but remember that it's a ½ penny for each of those things you may call jokes, because I never laughed. It comes to about 6d all round.

Richie This is an ant it will run about my bed just now.

This is a mosquito, just getting to work. I always leave one hole in my net to test his ingenuity & so as not to disappoint the clever ones.

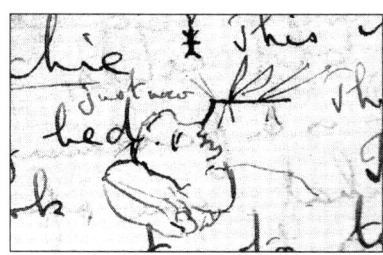

Pom Your account of the journey is excellent. I'm sorry about the Primus, the grice was evidently just ripe. I wonder if some stamps I sent you ever reached. I think some of my letters miss fire, so if ever you or anyone else happens to receive one just let me know.

I see you put too little on the F.B. so did Tommy & it cost me 4d but it was worth it.

Irene Yours is a good letter, so is the calendar which gave me much surprise & great joy when I opened it this morning. The monkey we have just now is great fun, but he do smell that bad & he will rummage in my hair, so far with little result!

I'm going to try to get a parrot but I doubt whether I can bring either of them home. I await the letter you promise. How's your writing, no I won't say that, but it's getting quite like Willie's.

With love to you all from your affectionate brother.

Leonard's K Elmhirst.

From Willie. 　　　　　　　　　　Rugeley Camp,
　　Capt Commdg. 'D' Compy.,　Stafford.
　　9th Batt. E. York. Regt.　　　20.2.1916.

To The Family.

It is with many regrets that I take my pen in hand again to apologise (I mean) for the War Budget's behaviour. He stowed himself away so securely that I'd almost forgotten him until he turned up during a fit of tidiness on my part. You see I've followed Tommy's example & am practising economy. I hope you like the colour. I'm afraid I've not got much news for you this time as its not long since I last wrote, besides you all saw me in January, except Leonard, & that ought to last you at least six months, I should think.

Nothing has happened here, except that 70 more recruits have come to my Company, a Zep flew over my head the other day & it gets muddier and muddier & I am to spend a night or two in the trenches this week with some of my men. Why I don't know. The trenches we propose spending 48 hours in, aren't half finished yet, no dugouts of any sort, & the weather lately has been awful. Frost, snow, rain & wind in turn & I believe we've only got a very few braziers to take with us to keep warm so don't be surprised if you hear of me being found by a faithful hound frozen at my post like Casabianca.

The Colonel suggested that I should make out my programme of work for next week (it goes on to the Brigade who are making us do this) as follows:- Monday & Tuesday – In the Trenches. Wed. Thurs. Fri. & Sat. – In Hospital.

The Zep went over our heads the night of the big raid but it was so dark we couldn't see it. It was about 11.30 p.m. & we seem to manufacture mud in some parts of the camp. I was hunting for a man this afternoon in some Pines about a mile away, & the mud was splashing in continually over the tops of my gum boots, & once or twice I nearly lost a boot. I unearthed or rather unmuddied the man's quarters at last but he wasn't in. I expect probably he had been drowned on his own doorstep & I walked over him without knowing.

As things are at present I shall probably be a fixture here for the duration of the war. I've tried various ways of getting away but none have been a success. One of my recruits pretended to be dumb when he first came & went on hunger strike. However he gave himself away the third day by answering my Q.M.S.[1] who asked him how much of his pay he wanted to allot to his mother each week. Then after five days he got tired of his hunger strike, & though still rather weak is recovering. He was very much annoyed because when he reported sick each morning, as he did, the doctor gave him "Medicine & Duty" instead of No Duty or Light Duty, so he had to go on parades & swallow some most unpleasant concoction into the bargain.

A letter has just reached me from Leonard this morning. He wrote it in November 1915 but forgot to put my Regt. on it & the Post Office have returned it to the Indian Dead Letter Office, so take warning & when you write to me each week don't forget the Regt.

All the convalescent Officers & men of our 6th 7th & 8th Batts. come back here when they're improving & stop till they're ready to go out again, so we get some good yarns. One Officer went into the dugout of a chap in another Regt. one day and noticed that he'd got a pair of boots put high up on one side of it and was using them as hat pegs. He said, "What an extraordinary place to keep your boots." "Oh," said the owner, "those aren't mine, they belong to the former tenant". Do you get the point? Some of the stories are a trifle "grewsome".

"How tired I am!" Just had dinner 1.0 p.m. six courses – "How full I am". I'm rather hoping to go over to Stancliffe for a couple of days this week if I can manage it. I got a card from Mr. Clarke a few days ago wanting to know when I was going. Now for the love & kisses.

<u>Leonard</u> I'm sorry to hear of your over-indulgence on Christmas Day. I hope it won't occur again. I'll try & reply to your letter sometime.

<u>Tommy</u> Don't break other things as well as records.

---

1 Quarter Masters Sergeant.

<u>Vic</u> Talk about early school at 7.0 a.m. I am out on parade at 6.45 & take my little lot for three quarters of an hour of marching & doubling on icy roads. We met five deer the other morning out for their run.

<u>Richard</u> Looks as if you had been writing letters in form judging by the paper you use. I've changed my address again you see but not my place of residence this time. I've not had the police after me lately.

<u>Alfred</u> I've not got anything to say to you I wrote you a letter the other day & you've not answered it yet.

<u>Irene</u> So glad to hear from Mother today that Conusy Wonusy has been cleaned. I won't tell the others what you caught off or on him last time I was at home & you <u>said</u> he was quite all right. Have you got Dash right yet? Your last letter was quite a good effort for a little girl. Any chickens yet? I won't write any more as it might cost another penny. 'How glad I am' that that's done now for another three or four months.

Much love to you all from your loving brother

William

From Richie. C/o C.E.M.Hawkesworth,
Rugby.
15th May 1916.

Dear Family,

Mr F.B., after having had a good rest cure, will no doubt run round the family with renewed speed. This is the first time I have seen it this year. I arrived here on the 11th inst as the result of the Rugby War economies, my luggage came on after me. I had to run to catch my train, it was a very hot day and I was wearing my overcoat. I look very severe now with spectacles. I went to the range today and shot much better though my right shoulder hurts a bit.

I believe Auntie Frances is paying a visit tomorrow. She is staying quite close. Leonard seems to like little animals in his bed what with ants and mosquitoes. There is nothing to write about. I went to Coumes with Irene last Monday, we had a fine time (?) We started off in style, it was nice and warm, but when we got to Mrs Hayward's it was starting to drizzle. When we got to the wood it was raining fairly hard. We ate our lunch under the nice holly bush below our usual lunching place. Then we started for the top of the wood by the other farm.

I climbed up to a nest from which Pom got 5 eggs and I got two babies. They were very small so I ------, we buried them. Then Irene climbed up to another nest. It was like climbing up a pair of steps, nothing in it. Then I went up one above the white cottage. The rain was running down the tree so when I swarmed up I dried the tree quite nicely with my trousers. Then we walked down to Mrs Hayward's and started off on our bicycles. I was nice and sticky. When we got nearly home, it had stopped raining. In fact we had quite an enjoyable time. Miss Allport's sausage dog is much bigger than Nan's, it gets rather a bad time.

We had a half holiday today because one of our masters has got the D.S.O. I am still in Mister Charlie Chaplin's (Charteris) form. Auntie Frances has just been here with Mrs Ramsbottom. I took them out to tea. We had our first Corps parade today. We are learning what the guards do, dressing, slow march etc. It is rather hard. I will try and write more when F.B. comes again, but I have written to Leonard and seen all the rest.

Willie. I hope you blew up Eyres into the air. Don't make remarks about my paper, yours is much worse.

Leonard. Give us particulars about the black buck, did you cut its throat with the knife?

Tommy. Remember that photo and don't make too many references about it.

Vic. You slacker, I hope you have sent a letter to Pom for F.B.

Pom. Thanks for your letter. How's the cash? Also, how is your friend Mr Feather? Has Mr Little asked you out yet?

Irene. I saw you just now; any more apoplectic victims yet?

All. Much love from your loving brother,

Richard Elmhirst.

From Alfred.   Chernocke House,
                                      Winchester.
                                      21st May 1916.

Dear Brethren,

I hope this leaves and reaches you as it does me. Vic couldn't say that could he? Well I should like to know why Vic did not contribute his share. I am sure it would not take him four months to write a letter. Well, I don't think we shall quite cry over the loss!!! We've been doing nothing exciting this week or last. I've had to play cricket every half-holiday this term, it's quite good fun, but one gets no time to ones' self which is the only drawback. I made 13 for a cup on Tuesday and 5 for another cup on Thursday. I keep wicket for the under 16's and House 2nd XI. I have caught one and stumped about half a dozen people.

We are having simply lovely weather here, much too hot to play cricket. I am in Chapel Choir[1] now and wear a surplice on Sundays. There are only eight trebles allowed in out of the whole school. I am wondering if my treble voice will go on as long as Leonards. I believe he still sings treble!

My 'toyes' look very smart. I have got a pair of cats with smiling faces which I have named Tweedledum and Tweedledee, a blackbird which I have named Tweaktum and a cow which used to hold matches, but which now makes an awfully good ink stand. I am going to take some photographs this afternoon.

Now for some sarcastic remarks, or otherwise:

<u>Willie</u>. I certainly answered your letter. I do wish you would send me your photo, if you have got any money to spare!! I must say that you had some rather good stories.

<u>Leonard</u>. At last your long wished for Act has arrived, the "Light saving" Bill. I remember when you told me about it on Hindhead Hill in Surrey,

---

[1] It is pleasing to note that a Barnsley tailor, Jack Heppenstall, was commissioned a few years ago to provide new gowns for the choristers of Winchester College.

on that leave out day. Didn't we just have a good time. I am so sorry about those stamps, but I think it must have been waylaid because I answered it the same week I got it.

Tommy. You must try and come down here some time this term. If you are staying near London you can get awfully good trains, or Airship of course. There is a very good place for landing in our fields!!!

Vic. I think it's time Uncle Jim might write a letter soon!!

Richie. No luck yet with Mr Little, but I shook hands with him at the beginning of term which sounds hopeful. Mr Bathe's still going strong.

Irene. I'm awfully sorry about F.B. but the butler put the stamp on. I'll see that he does it right this time. Well I hope the animals are like Johnny Walker.

Much love to everybody from

Your loving brother Alfred. O. Elmhirst.

P.S. I hope the photos, although bad prints, will be appreciated.

From Irene Rachel. Pindar Oaks Hall
Barnsley,
23rd May 1916.

Dear Family,

At last, after a prolonged rest, the old F.B. has come this way again, but I also should like to know why Vic has not put anything in. Quite a lot has happened since the hols and more still since I wrote in F.B. We have been having some really hot weather and so we have teas outside and are playing croquet, also going to the swimming baths. Since the new lighting regulations Miss Coleclough and I have tennis after supper.

Yesterday there was quite an excitement, two dogs came into the field and Daddy raced after them and had a shot from the tennis ground and "tickled them up" a bit. Then one of them came again and Daddy came out, but it was too far down the field to reach.

May 26th. We went to the swimming baths yesterday and had great fun there. There were only two other people. I have quite a lot of chicks. From Mr Clarke's prize sitting only 6 have come out, but there was a chick in every one only they were so weak that they could not peck themselves out, but the six are very strong. I have got a few bants but they have not all come out yet. Poor Conus gets such frights. There is a very fierce old lady in the back yard which gave him beans the other day chasing along the path and down the slips so now he takes care and treats all with due respect!!

John Willie is not dead yet and sings very nicely. He came out onto the tea table when we were having tea near the window and was so funny, he hopped onto the bread and butter, then onto the sugar basin! Two men came last night to the pond and drowned a wretched dog in it. It has not been taken out yet. I expect most of you know that Spider has been sold to Mr Wood and just takes the milk round. We see her now and again in Ouslethwaite Park. Pindar is just being trained and his mouth is healed up after having the funny bit on. He gets driven about the field and now goes onto the road and is getting quite good with trams and doesn't mind motors much. The first time Johnson took him onto the road he said he nearly jumped into a shop window when a tram came by rather fast as only about one older man in another tram will stop for him. Miss Coleclough and I had a very good game of tennis yesterday. We had marked the lines, but of course it has to rain today.

<u>Willie.</u> I wish you would stop making nasty remarks about Scon. I am getting rather tired of hearing them! Your little bits of weed that you brought from Aunt Fanny's are doing very well. There was, so I believe, a hen on it a little time ago only she did no damage!! My garden is doing very well and the sweet peas are very well; better than Kitsons, so there! Even though you say there won't be any flowers on it as they are under the laburnums.

<u>Leonard.</u> I am glad you liked my letter. It took a lot of writing and don't say horrid things about my writing, what about your own. Do you ever give Mickey a bath? Praps if you did he would not smell so bad! Give a lot of pats to Kim for me and the monkey a pull of the tail.

<u>Tommy.</u> I am glad the motor bike is going again alright. Of course, now as you have it going you might go over to Port Patrick and see about my mac.

<u>Vic.</u> As there is not a letter from you I cannot answer anything, but I hope you will get to Stonehenge and by this time I expect your ankle will be alright again.

<u>Richie.</u> Glad you have got your gogs. I hope they feel nice. You should not go and say that the tree was like a pair of steps, it was quite a hard climb!! Of course, none of your cheek.

<u>Pom.</u> The bulk of the animals are very well, like Johnny Walker. You seem to be getting on, what with shooting and a new bat!!

Well, I must now close this "lengthy epistle".

From your loving sister,

Irene.

From Tommy. Naval Airship Station,
Luce Bay,
Stranraer.
7th June 1916.

Dear Family,

As it is a very short time since I saw you all except Leonard, who I wrote to a few days ago so I have very little to say. Things go on very much the same here, some weeks flying every day and some not at all. Last week nothing owing to high winds the whole time. We have started playing cricket here but have not yet got a pitch so it is limited to nets of which we have bought one and a piece of coconut matting, which makes for very good practice. We have also started a little tennis on non-flying evenings, but the nearest courts are seven and eight miles away which makes it rather difficult. However, a motor-bike and these long evenings are helpful.

I should have left here a month ago but things move very slowly so I don't know really when it will be, but I hope as soon as possible.

I hope that none of you thought that the Navy had been beaten when you saw the first report of the Jutland battle[1], though it was rather a startler. Two of us here having come from the Battle Cruiser Squadron guessed at once what had happened, but most of the people round had a pretty bad shock. I only wish I had been there myself.

<u>Willie</u>: Hope the jaundice has passed away.

<u>Leonard</u>: Next time you are home you must try my present motor-bike, an Indian. It goes fine now but of course it may be broken by then.

<u>Vic</u>: This ought to miss you really as you missed it last time. I hear you are becoming great at cricket, also at falling off walls, at any rate, that is better than off bikes.

---

1   This was a famous encounter off Jutland between the British Grand Fleet commanded by Admiral Sir John Jellicoe and the German High Seas Fleet commanded by Admiral von Steer. The battle disappointed the British public, but it made the Germans realise that they could not win such daylight encounters.

Richard: Sorry about the photo. At any rate it looks better than yours in gig-lamps.

Alfred: I hear you are doing great things at cricket. That must be my coaching on the tennis lawn.

Irene: I believe you have the orac now. Do you want any ferrets, we have 12 here and two owls.

Best of luck to all from your affectionate brother

Thomas Elmhirst.

From Leonard.	Emily Lodge,
	Nanii Jal,
	India.
	16th Sept 1916.

Dear Family.

Now that you are all dispersed once more, it is time for me to take pen and send this off. At the moment most of you, I suppose, are gricing[1] and I am hoping for long and vivid accounts by the next mail.

Since my last of Jan 1st, I have travelled some thousands of miles. A four day train journey with a few halts on the way took me down to Kodaikanal, a little place 7000 feet sheer up on the top of some hills in the South of India. English flowers and climate, a lake with boats, a few picnics, mostly with Americans who are just first rate cookers of all kinds of sweets, buns, beans, Indian corn and other combustibles.

I was supposed to be learning shorthand and typewriting with a view to becoming a private secretary to our general secretary who is now on his way to England to help in taking charge of the Y.M.C.A. in Britain and France. Name - Carter, an American with all the corners rubbed off, who can sum up your worth in a five minutes conversation.

Then to Bangalore, quite a pleasant place in Mysore where I lived on curry and rice for a whole week and enjoyed it. I also played football and met many interesting young Indians – three weeks in Poona, the home of my American tutor and much sedition, which the government seem incapable of squashing – You don't teach a child to draw by taking away his pencil because his first effort is rather a failure. But still, all Government officials are not so short sighted.

I was on the edge of becoming one myself a few days ago. The director of Public Instruction for the United Provinces and my cousin Ted Richardson (very distant) pressed me to accept a job either as lecturer in history at a college in Allahabad, or (don't laugh) headmaster of a High

---

1   "Gricing". Family slang for grouse shooting.

School, which is like a Public School out here. Salary about £400 a year, rising to anything later on with a pension at the end and a nice house, plenty of holidays too in which to read, study or hunt. Very attractive wasn't it. But in spite of the fact that my last job is off owing to Carter going back to Europe immediately, they have found me another job which sounds interesting in Poona and at present they won't let me go.

After three weeks in Poona and a two days journey across the peninsula I arrived in what is probably the one other place that you could put your finger to in India without looking at the map, besides Bombay. Calcutta, consists of a fascinating river with wonderful prehistoric boats and barges, a pontoon bridge, a huge grass park, a long street and some Government buildings which remind one of London and a squalid city of cheap houses with a wonderfully interesting dirty and smellful Indian quarter. There is a large Eurasian or Anglo-Indian population also, i.e. half black half white, – chocolate creams they are known as by the Indian who despises them because they will have nothing to do with him and try to ape the European.

I found Calcutta a most depressing place. I was working hard and knew very few people there, then I got dengue fever which, after a week, leaves you unable to walk or to stand. This combined with the fact that my efforts to learn shorthand and typing were wasted and that I was jobless wrought an extremely pessimistic state of mind, which was only cured by getting away here, up in the hills among hospitable kindly relations, cool air instead of steam, sunshine, English food and customs. Here I sit and read and sketch and write.

Tea and fruit at 7 am, a walk up to the top of a very jungly hill which rises up straight at the back of the house before breakfast at 9. I got my first view of the Himalayas, (pronounced Him-arl-iers) –beautiful snow capped peaks many miles away.

The newly discovered cousins are so nice and as there are two other visitors we have great fun. Tennis we get quite a lot of up here too. In India, except Calcutta, all the grounds are gravel and you always have at least three men or boys (chokras) to field and hand you the balls, a lazy way. There are no roads here only endless paths and the only means of conveyance is either pony-back or dandy, a cradle kind of thing with a pole at each end and two cross pieces held on the shoulders of four hill men. They get over the ground very quickly.

One of the peculiarities of India is the bath or (gussel). It is never anything more than a zinc tub, such as you wash clothes in at home. Only a few of the best hotels have a proper English bath. I am provided with a servant here – most embarrassing I found it at first. Even now I rather dislike his attentions – he pops your shirt over your head, holds out your trouser legs so that you can shoot your foot through with ease, swings the braces over your shoulders from the back and fastens the back buttons whilst you do the front, puts your shoes on and tries to do them up. I struck at that. Then he holds your coat and waistcoat and in the intervals stands and watches you tie your tie and brush your hair with great interest.

Leopards live in the back garden. Also beautiful silvery monkeys with black faces called Langurs and martens. I've only seen the monkeys so far. Now for a few remarks.

Willie: The best of luck and come back safe. I think I owe you a letter.

Tommy: Send me a photo and a few particulars about the larger airship. Have you discovered the secret of the Zeppelin yet? How's the Indian bike?

Victor: Did I hear it whispered that you had conquered Stonehenge? I feel that not even the taking of Caubles in the near future can beat this.

Richard: You ask for particulars of the blackbuck; with luck you will see them at home. I got a man who was returning to take home two stuffed heads and the skull. Two are proper blackbuck, the other is a chink, with very good horns.

Pom: How is Pym, have you seen him lately? Send me a photo of yourself. Many congratulations on the singing effort. Get a record made and send it out.

Irene: I'm trusting you to try and get the others to write to me now and then. You don't know how dismal it is to get only one letter by the mail. Look carefully and you'll find my remark about your writing was not nasty but a compliment. I do miss Nickey and Kim so much.

Your affectionate Leonard.

A children's party at Round Green in 1906. Pom in the foreground, Richie, cousins Jack and Cecil, Vic, Tommy and Irene Rachel.

Irene Rachel tending her pigs at Pindar Oaks.

Christie, Tommy (with net) and Vic in 1903.

Irene Rachel on one horse, Pom, Richie, Vic and Tommy on another horse with Christie standing by. 1910?

The older Elmhirst generation in front of Elmhirst. From left to right: Marjorie Mann (Auntie Min), Uncle Charles, Fanny Elmhirst (Auntie Fan) Herbert Elmhirst (Uncle Bert), William Heaton Elmhirst (Papa) and Aunt Edith. 1887.

Elmhirst, Worsbrough, Barnsley. Built in 1860–62 for the Rev. William Elmhirst and demolished in 1948 due to mining subsidence after the death of the Rev. W. H. Elmhirst.

Willie teaching Irene Rachel how to fence.

Vic, Richie, Pom and Irene Rachel.

The whole family at Pindar Oaks. 1911.

*The whole family plus cousins and Grand-Mama Elmhirst.
From front left to right: Vic, Tommy, Leonard, Richie, Grand-Mama (holding cousin Cecil) cousin Jack and Christie.
In the back row are Irene Rachel and Pom on the donkey (Pom was cross because he thought he should have the front seat), cousins Marjorie and Nan Mann (daughters of Auntie Min).*

A family group in 1915 including Papa and Mama, Irene Rachel, Vic, Richie, Aunt Francis Knight, cousin Marjorie Mann and friend.

Irene Rachel on a raft in Pindar Oaks colliery pond with brothers Richie and Vic in attendance. 1909.

All the children assembled on a ladder at Pindar Oaks. 1910.

Shooting party at Lassintullich in 1915.
Front row: Richie, Conus, Pom and Irene Rachel.
Middle: Uncle Bertie, Mama and Papa (Never, never let your gun pointed be at anyone!)
Back row: Vic, Leonard, Tommy and Campbell the Ghillie.

At the wedding of Anne G. Elmhirst (Jack's daughter) to Dick Garmons-Williams in 1950.
Back row: Vic, Gwen, Pom, Irene Rachel, Leonard and Tommy.
Front row: Richard N. Elmhirst, Paul B. Elmhirst and Tisha Barker.

Pom, Leonard and Richie sharing Pom's Triumph motorbike. (Two aunts behind)

Leonard, cousin Jack, cousin Cecil, Pom, Richie and Irene Rachel at Elmhirst in 1918.

Papa contemplates the meaning of farm modernisation while Pom, Maurice Telford and George Hayhurst sort out the plough.

Houndhill, Worsbrough, Barnsley. (Built by Roger Elmhirst circa 1599 then fortified by Richard Elmhirst during the Civil War).

From Willie.   Somewhere in France
                                Oct. 26th 1916

Dear Family,

Many thanks for the F.B. which reached me last Friday night at the First Army School where I spent five pleasant weeks, though quite energetic. I'm now back with the Battalion under canvas – in a wood, a couple of miles or so behind the line, farther south than when I left them last month. As for the mud here, Rugeley Camp was nothing to it. I was out both yesterday and today from 11 to 5 with 200 men road clearing and draining! Every wagon and lorry that goes past sprinkles you from head to foot & the roads round here just now are getting about as much traffic if not more on them in the 24 hours than the New Road[1] does in a week & large caterpillars & other queer beasts are rather worse than tractions.

Talk about trains being late at Grandtully, it's nothing to what they are here. It took me three days to travel a hundred miles. At one place where I changed the 4.40 a.m. train didn't go until 1 p.m.! & we had to wait about all that time as no one could tell us when it would go. After that we spent a whole day (24 hours) five in a carriage with all our luggage, valises and everything & hadn't a proper meal the whole time.

Well I must finish off now as its 10.15 p.m. & tomorrow morning I'm parading at 6.30 to go up to the trenches for 48 hours, in a rather unhealthy spot. I haven't seen a tank yet but probably shall do in a day or two.

Well love to everybody from your affect. brother

William

---

1 An improved section of the main road from Barnsley to Sheffield before the M1 was built.

In Memory of

Captain W Elmhirst

8th Bn., East Yorkshire Regiment
who died aged 24 on Monday, 13th November 1916.

Captain Elmhirst, Son of the Rev. W. H. Elmhirst, of
"Elmhirst", Barnsley, Yorks. Educated at Malvern College
and Worcester College, Oxford.

Remembered with honour
SERRE ROAD CEMETERY No. 1, Pas de Calais, France.

In the perpetual care of
the Commonwealth War Graves Commission

Willie's "In Memoriam" Information.

From Richie.   C/o C.E.M.Hawkesworth,
                                Rugby.
                                10th February 1917.

Dear Family,

Once again F.B. has arrived after the longest delay. Vic kept it for a short time and did not send a letter and this time keeps it. The next time he will not send it at all I expect. He is also slightly inaccurate as to the journey he took me to Huddersfield. I said it's only a paltry 12 miles, we can do it in 15 minutes. It was really quite fifteen and, not being a competent chauffeur, the tool box (where the Johnson implement is kept) was not properly fastened and I had to hold it there with my stick. We reached Huddersfield Station as the train went out and a porter, who took me for a poor little boy I think, told me "Oh yes, a train at 4.15 gets to Rugby at 6.15" (my ordinary train gets in at 7.20). So I started off in style and only had to change four times, waiting ¾ of an hour at a wayside station and at last getting to Rugby at 9.14. without my luggage which came a week later.

I am in the best study in the house which Hawker says is the shop-window and we have got it because we are the tidiest people. I also got out of my form this term and my form master is the O.C. of the O.T.C. He is very sarcastic. I am also a lance corporal in the Bugle Band besides being one in the corps proper. (What must the corps at Marlborough be like now? They do do some funny things) I am in the house quartet this term and also in the House Shout. We have played no rugger yet this term. I have been for one "bumph" chase and several ordinary runs, but since Sat Jan 27th we have had nothing except skating and tobogganing. We had a half on the next Monday when I hired a pair of skates for the week which consisted of four whole afternoons skating. On Sunday there was deep snow and on Tuesday we had very good tobogganing. On Wednesday we were excused two lessons and we had lunch at 12.30. On Thursday the tobogganing was not very good, but the skating today, where the snow had been brushed off, was quite good.

We have already started getting down to our 4 lbs of bread etc for the week. We are not starved yet. I believe I am going farming when the snow has gone. The school has bought 12 acres of land to grow potatoes in. We break up on Wednesday April 4th and return on May 3rd. And now after a few terse sayings I will conclude my letter.

Leonard. I admired the blackbuck head greatly and at Christmas, with a bit of holly tied to one ear, he looked decidedly pretty.

Tommy. Have you got the complete Zep yet to bring home? My bits are on my mantelpiece. How's the mud and rugger? They should combine well.

Vic. I have said something about you. I spoke to our Prior the other day. He remarked that if you were in his brother's house you would be kept inside. You are extraordinarily filthy and there is no excuse.

Pom. Why don't cher nock? How's the "tweaker"? I find that it is, or used to be, a Rugby word fifty years ago used by Selous.

Irene. Where's my calendar? Is J.B. alive or has he been killed by Sir D.?

Much love and best wishes from Richard Elmhirst.

From Irene Rachel.

Pindar Oaks,
Barnsley.
18th March 1917.

Dear Family, At last, F.B. comes round again after a prolonged reading with old Iron Shins[1]. There has been quite a lot happening this term what with skating etc. Miss Coleclough and I had very good skating on the pond here and also at Stainbro' with Auntie Min and Marjorie. One day here Daddy tried and Aunt Edie. She got on quite well and did not go down once!! Conus enjoyed himself very much, we had to be careful not to skate on his toes and Tory was very funny galloping round after us, but in the end he always gave it up.

When Pom came home for a fortnight or so we got in quite a lot of rabbiting. We had just got two new ferrets and they were <u>very</u> bitey. One used to come at us open mouthed and make great snaps. The first morning they went out, Pom and I, after many futile attempts, at last got them into the box and off they went in the "old red tub". Of course I <u>had</u> to stop at home and do lessons !!! so I only heard about it afterwards. Oh, I forgot to say, while hunting the ferrets round their hutch to get them, I got a luscious bite on my finger. My goodness us, it did hurt.

After about the first stick heap the bitie one got Pom's finger and he danced a jig waving it in the air till it was shaken off and sent flying, it unfortunately landed against a piece of wood and stunned it a bit but it did not stun its bitieness worse luck. Also, Daddy got a bite.

But now they are getting quite good, though they were rather a long time in some stick heaps at Round Green at the quarry plantation. When we had to go in lots for tea at Auntie Min's, Tommy went off back to "watch and wait" after having had a bite and a sup, but in the end we got them. I pulled the last one out with the help of some rabbit stuffing. (Leonard, you will be glad to know I unstuffed one by myself!) And Pom, while he was here used to get the ferret 'game' of some kind just about every day, either a starling or two or a sparrow or blackbird. He and I and Conus

---

1 "Iron shins". The family nickname for Vic.

used to watch the tussle in their wire cage and when they tried to get through the hole into their hut it was too funny to see them stick because the hole was not large enough for both of them to get through!!

Gladys has been staying for some time here, nearly three weeks. It was lovely having them again, we had great fun. One afternoon we all went spreading manure in our field at Ouslethwaite, Gladys, Miss Coleclough, Pom and I. We have been very busy with that field. A few days ago, after getting all the small fruit trees up that Daddy has planted here, we took them up to Elmhirst to plant in Pindar Oaks orchard, which is one end of the tennis ground as we do not want two tennis grounds. I have not seen them in yet as, after leaving them there, Miss C and I sailed off in the cart with old Doc, <u>me</u> driving, to the field to do more manuring. At quarter to five we harnessed up and jogged home.

On Tuesday afternoon we went again with Vic. Miss C and he spread while I dragged with Doctor. One Saturday, Daddy, Pom, Doctor and I took up all the bees to Elmhirst. We made two journeys and now they are all nicely settled in the corner with one side to the tennis ground and the other to the frames and their fronts to the greenhouse.

Conus is quite well, he had <u>two</u> washes in one week; I don't know quite why, but he was none the worse. Also Bruce is very well. A little while ago, when Daddy was at Elmhirst, he left him and was away all that night. Daddy told the police and he went round to different places looking for him. Then that evening before dinner a man brought him back from Dodworth. He had gone to Mr Thorley, the old tenant of Lewdin Farm, at his farm there and had slept most of the day there.

<u>Leonard</u>: I hope you get plenty of letters now. And I should think by this time you have got the parcel with the toffee etc in by now. Many thanks for films which arrived on Saturday. I will send prints as soon as possible.

<u>Tommy</u>: I do want to see your little car. I hope you will bring it over soon; and of course, you could bring some petrol too!! Is the cat all right? And do my drawings look nice in your cabin? Send me some more and one of ------J.B.- how did you like my last batch? – Say if you didn't.

<u>Vic</u>: I have not a ferret skin rug in my room, nor am I likely to have one, unless you go skinning them or something. And Conus, as I have said before, is very well and never has --------; I won't say what because I expect you know what they are like; when you go sleeping in your clothes and such like dirty tricks.

<u>Richie</u>: You say, "Where's your calendar?" Why, I should say it is hanging in your study. I should look if I were you. As for dear J.B., I had just about forgotten him. He is very well but now that Sir Douglas has gone back he cannot try to fight him.

<u>Pom</u>: The ferrets do miss you I am sure. They never get any game now. I hope your 'Toyes' look nice. Aunty Fan and Aunt Edie have just left Elmhirst and are staying for a few days at the Rookery till Daddy is quite ready. They came back from church this morning with Daddy, Mother and Vic. Miss Coleclough and I went up to Elmhirst and found two little boys with big bunches of snowdrops and chased them but they jumped the wall at the bottom of the quarry and we did not get them- worse luck.

With love from your loving sister Irene.

From Tommy.

Royal Airship Station
Howden.
E. Yorks.
1st April 1917

Dear Family,

Once again the Budget was round, very much delayed en route at Marlbrough, but as it will not go there next time round, we will hope to see it again in less than six months. I have not much to put in this time, so cannot write much, however I have done a lot of flying this year, over a hundred hours already, which is not bad for an airship in winter. I am afraid I cannot send a photo of it round, as they have not yet been published officially, but I will hope to put one in next round.

Tommy as a Captain of his airship P5 (see top left figure) at Howden around 1917-18.

We are in the midst of a snow storm today, in fact there is a drift three foot deep outside my window now. Not a very good entry for April. I have just bought a car, and am trying to sell the Brough motorbike to help to pay for it. I advertised it last week and have already had 8 applications, so should have no difficulty. The car, which I expect most of you will have seen, before this gets to you, is a 14 H.P. Crossley, a large two seater, with seats for two more behind if necessary. It has wire wheels and looks quite smart but has rather too much brasswork for my liking. I expect it will get painted all over before long.

We are trying hard to make cricket and tennis grounds here for the summer, but they take a deal of making out of hay fields but if we are going to have much fine weather in summer I doubt we shall not have much time to play. The mess seems to get fuller of dogs, I left my cabin door open the other night before turning in and came in later to find a very dirty retriever puppy lying on my pyjamas and pillow and clean sheets. I am afraid I rather forcibly ejected him.

I am hoping to remain here all summer, but don't know where I shall go after that, most probably to a British Zep ? but we hope the war will be nearly over by then.

I am afraid I have no photos to put in, but will try to get one of Laxton Vicarage from the air to put in next time this comes round.

With much love to you all

from your affect. brother

Thomas W Elmhirst

From Alfred. Chernocke House,
Winchester.
April 1917.

Dear Family,

What a welcome sight old F.B. was to me this morning at breakfast, it's simply years since I last saw him, we have 'Old Iron Shins' to thank for that. Anyhow, here it is at last. I have been trying to keep a diary this year. I have forgotten it for the last few days though.

I have had quite a lot of soccer this term and play for the house under 16, for which I have scored quite a few goals. We went on playing although the frost came and made the ground, (as Vic says, like a rock) until a chap in our house was 'knotted' over and broke his arm; he was in our house, so then they stopped footer.

Since then I have skated nearly every day and am making quite good progress. I can skate backwards and do an outside and inside edge!! We have a splendid stretch of water meadows to skate on. The ice was rather spoilt by the snow that came. Still some places have been swept and it is jolly good fun. I have been having some awfully good games of ice-hockey, it's jolly good fun. It has begun to thaw now and when you fall down on the ice you get soaked to the skin. I will continue tomorrow as I have to go to bed now.

To resume, I have just got back from skating 6 miles away, it was great fun, we weren't sure that the ice would bear, but it was all right. Mumps is raging through the whole school and a good many have got pneumonia, so that two houses have all gone home. We have got one case of mumps in our house and a doubtful case of pneumonia. Everything that I did last term has gone clean out of my mind. It was such a long time since I had F.B., it is nearly a year ago.

We went for a march out this afternoon, rather a long one, I was in the attacking party so had to go the longest way, but it was not bad fun. I'm afraid I've no photos to spare at present as I stuck them all in a book.

We are getting off all work before breakfast now till the frost goes and it is a nice change, although we have to do extra work to make up for it. I've got a fine painting of John Bull in my 'toyes[1]' done by I.R.E. I'm expecting a calendar any time this term, which I saw last holidays, but which had no calendar part to it, painted by the same artist!!

I am a two year man now which means I needn't go to 'heres[2]' which are shouted by a prefect when he wants anything, and the last person is taken. It is a great relief and you can watch other people going to 'heres' and it gives you much pleasure. I have just had a long letter from Leonard at Basra. He is very well and by the time he gets this I hope I shall have answered it. If I don't I will thank you for it now. By the way, now I'm a two year man I'm allowed to have the gramophone out whenever I like!!

Leonard: Pym left some time ago. I don't know where he is now. I'll spare you a record of my solo, I don't think the gramophone would record it!!

Tommy: It's time you came down here to see me. Mr Broomfield says he will put you up. He doesn't know what he is undertaking does he.

Vic: I've just remembered, I think it was 42 wasn't it. It strikes me you think a deal too much of all your captaincy and sergeanting. I don't quite see how you can do both!! Miss Bishof was quite taken with Richie and me, she said, not with you though.

Richie: The tweaker is going strong and hasn't bust yet. I'm in an awful dilemma.

Irene: The old washerwoman with the spring lead is fine and the horses as well. You seem to be getting on well with your skating. Rumour here says that the whole school is going home!!

Well, I must close now with all my love and best wishes to everybody from your loving brother Alfred. O. Elmhirst.

P.S. My new signature A.O.E. – Rather good isn't it.

---

1   "Toyes". Winchester slang for one's study.
2   "Heres". The Winchester call for a fag. (a junior boy to run an errand.)

From Leonard.   Y.M.CA.
                                      Basrah. IEF."D"
                                      5th June 1917.

Dear Family,

Never did the old F.B. get such a hearty welcome after so lengthy an absence. But the defaulter has made up for it well. Besides a cunning pen and ink sketch from the hands of the famous bird artist I have a lengthy extract from his private "log" which shall be included in the F.B. and a long letter for myself. But in spite of this it is unseemly that such delays should recur in our well regulated circulation.

I hope to celebrate the fatal morrow by drawing to a close His Majesty's liberal and extensive hospitality. Needless to say my friend George always does things handsomely and our last nights homely fare was washed down with a bottle of Japanese pale ale.

It is nearly six months since I last wrote I believe – and much has happened since. I spent three months providing entertainment and refreshments at a low cost in one of the most unhealthy spots in the country. It was brought to a close by an order at an hours notice to proceed to a camp out on the desert and take the place of a man who had quarrelled with his O.C. The said O.C. (may you be spared a meeting with him) was once a military prison commandant. I'd experienced one of the same sort in India. However, he happened to be a great friend of a deceased cousin of ours, a famous hunting man who always wrote the accounts of the 'Pytchley' pack for the Field under the name of Brooksby[1] and we would establish points of mutual contact on the matter of pigs and manures. He used to treat all the men as though they had been remanded and as a Camp Commandant he was thoroughly efficient. My word! If he saw

---

1   Edward Pennell Elmhirst wrote about hunting for The Field under the pen name of "Brooksby". He was a very colourful character and the nephew of General Charles Elmhirst. Although he was an army officer, he hunted in Japan, India, South Africa and in the far west of America as well as throughout England. He wrote several books on hunting. He is reputed to be the first winner of the Rugby shooting cup later won by Vic.

> **DETAILS OF "BROOKSBY."**
>
> Sir,—Captain Pennell-Elmhirst's biography, with steel-engraved portrait, appears in the November, 1895, issue of "Baily's Magazine." He was Leicestershire born, the son of the Rev. Edward Elmhirst, of Shawell Rectory, a notable sportsman in the cricket-field and a good shot and follower of hounds. "Brooksby" was educated at Rugby, and made the highest score for the school when she first won the Elcho Shield. He was entered to hounds under Charles Payne, but left school when seventeen years old, was gazetted to the 9th Foot, and went with it to China. In his twentieth year he was elephant-hunting in the Malay Peninsula, and went thence to Japan, where, with a pack of English dwarf foxhounds, he hunted every kind of quarry round Yokohama. During the return voyage round the Cape, Pennell-Elmhirst collaborated with a brother officer, Mounteney Jephson (afterwards author of "With the Colours"), in an initial literary venture, "Our Life in Japan," and soon afterwards began his connection with the "Field," then edited by "Stonehenge" (Mr. Walsh).
>
> For some years instructor of musketry in his battalion, Elmhirst accompanied his uncle, General C. Elmhirst, to Malta and afterwards to Mysore as aide-de-camp, and when in the former island he succeeded, with the help of his chief, in securing ground for polo, which has flourished there since. In India he enjoyed big game hunting, and chased the jackal with a pack of hounds from the Quorn, Pytchley, and Belvoir during the summer; and was granted leave to return home each winter to ride over Leicestershire (lucky man!).
>
> Finally, "Brooksby," who had now become permanent correspondent of the "Field" in "grass countries," was commissioned to describe "The Hunting Countries of England." His three works, "The Cream of Leicestershire," "The Best Season on Record" (1882-4), and "Foxhound, Forest, and Prairie," were published by Messrs. Routledge and Sons. The Rocky Mountains and Far West, the stiff timber fences of Long Island, and the Ward and Tipperary countries were all described by his pen as well as the Meath in John Watson's reign. Pennell-Elmhirst was Master of the Woodland Pytchley during the 1879-80 season. I am without information as to the date of his death.—Yours, &c., H. R. TATE.
>
> [To the above details we may add that "Brooksby" served in the second South African War (medal and two clasps). He also wrote "The Best of the Fun" (1908). He was born on January 7th, 1845, and died on December 2nd, 1916.—ED.]
>
> Sir,—I see that a correspondent is asking for biographical details of Captain Pennell-Elmhirst ("Brooksby"). I count it an honour to have known him pretty well, both in the hunting field and out of it, during the last ten years of his life, and could, I dare say, furnish some of the particulars required. He died at Blisworth, Northamptonshire, in 1916 at the age of seventy-one.
>
> If your correspondent happens to have access to the Foxhunting Volume of the Lonsdale Library (Seeley Service and Co.), for which I was responsible a few years ago, he will find a little appreciation of the man in Chapter XXXII.
>
> Mr. Lucas-Lucas, of Rugby, painted a most characteristic portrait of him on his old black horse, with Brooksby Church and hall, Tom Firr ("the central figure of my hunting life," as he termed him), and the Quorn hounds in the background. I have an engraving of it which a friend kindly gave me, but I do not know where there is another to be had, nor in whose possession the original is. I remember seeing it displayed a good many years ago in Messrs. Fores's window in Piccadilly.—Yours, &c., CHARLES FREDERICK.

Biographical account of Edward Pennell Elmhirst.

a matchstick on the floor of the canteen this sort of thing would happen: Enter orderly at salute, "Adj wishes to see you, 7.0 pm". Yours truly pulls up his socks, adjusts tie and curl over right ear and hurries off. Adj: "O.C. complains about lamps in your tent, are they properly shaded?" "Well Sir, I'm not sure what properly is, but they're just like the one on your table". (O.C. wasn't in but he'd been prying round evidently) It so happened that the lamp on the Adj's table was a "naked light" so I was O.K. and whether he passed it or no I'm not sure.

We really were on excellent terms, even though, with an eye to business he established a private canteen with rebait [sic], proposed putting up and running his own recreation hut and gave me orders to quit. I'd prepared for this and, as luck would have it, got a large piece of desert close to his camp, outside his control and within reach of half a dozen others, to do what I liked with. I spent three happy weeks there and once again ran wild in what I.R.E. would vulgarly call a scratch patch. It didn't quite blossom like a rose but had I had a chance there's no knowing what might have happened.

Owing to the kindness of my neighbours, tents sprang up like mushrooms. I got a fatigue party of 10 to put up a big double roof state marquee which holds 400 easily, a rope broke at the critical moment, & crash. The roof pole shod with iron was broken in two places. However, after many trials at last with 80 men on the job, we got it well established. With chlorinated water laid on and 100 lbs ice per day, we were able to supply an unlimited amount of iced lime juice and lemonade.

I invited the old C.O. over to inspect one Sunday afternoon – he was rather fed up because his supposed recreation hut had fallen through and his men were without a place of any kind inside his camp. Then he saw we'd got two new Hospital marquees up, – how had we got them? He'd ordered two weeks ago and they'd supplied us before him. So he took it out by flaring up because the men didn't stand to attention directly he walked into the canteen tent and he proceeded to curse me and a corporal. I quietly led him away, steered him clear of the other marquee with men in it and just before he left, explained that as a non-official I had no power or right to give an order at all and we parted quite amicably.

A previous secretary had borrowed some of his bed boards for a temporary platform and sawn their ends off and he had been very angry about it. However, we managed to replace them and the old ones made an excellent bandstand. As we were able to get a band three times a week, things began to be quite gay.

I was given just enough time to work out the main scheme, get to know all the useful people in the area and then with schemes for an open air stage, shower baths, a barber's shop and other items unrealised was packed off to fill the place at Amara. Our Baghdad Sec had fallen ill and owing to lack of men we had to have a regular General Post. Except at this time of year Amara, (and even now late in the evening and early in the morning) Amara is a delightful place, almost like an Indian station. Everything is fairly permanent and our Arab neighbours have quickly "docilated" under the British thumb, so that a club has been built where officers and sisters play tennis in the evening, (I'm on the committee but unfortunately it's just my busy time at the Y.M. when the sun goes down). Yesterday they even opened a desert golf club!

The river forks just here and the palms on the banks make it very picturesque. The population is largely composed of Sabians, numbers of whom are silver smiths. They are the followers of John the Baptist and descendants of his converts, have their own bishops and schools and are a very wealthy if diminutive community. Only two of the silver workers do really good work – inlaying black on silver – as far as I can gather a development of the old Damascene steel inlay work of the Middle Ages. I'll bring some home for you to see with luck.

As for the Arabs, they strike me as a delightful people, especially the children, who are very hard workers and always ready for a joke (or backsheesh). The Tommies who've met Arabs up the line won't agree here and there's no doubt that under Jim Turk's oppressive and disastrous regeime [sic], as well as during the change of masters, they've done a lot of very dirty work. And especially under Gorringe, were treated for it in Prussian manner. But gradually, as the troops pass on, the Political Officers, (i.e. The British civilising agency) take the place of the military, and diplomacy and tact take the place of summary execution and village destruction. The officers and soldiers will tell you how disastrous this is, rather naturally, having seen the Arab at his worst. The Political Officer will complain that the military go too far, because he's got to live with the Arab and turn him into a friendly civilised being. However, as I see it, there's little reason to think so far that either method has been carried too far. Certainly, the Arab seems to become a different being after a year of law and order under the British flag.

From the middle of May to the end of July we get it anything from 115 to 130 degrees in the shade and the order has just come out that between 8 and 4 no soldier is to work in the sun. In hospital we just lie and perspire freely, only we're lucky in having electric fans which go from 8 in the morning to 12 at night.

There are a fair number of troops here and there's a good deal to be done to set our various centres, (Six of them) on their legs. If all goes well and there's no front to go to, eventually up in this direction – well, I shall make a move elsewhere, always remembering that my return ticket is due in September, if there's a chance of being more useful elsewhere.

Anyhow, I hope that by the time this has seen you all the end will be nearer than in sight.

Your affectionate brother, Leonard K Elmhirst.

Supplement to F.B.

Tommy: Best luck with your new ship which you may have by this time, also with the car. Have just read Naval Occasions again, do you know it? Makes me want to join the Navy. Cook's boy or powder-monkey – what?

Vic: Many thanks for letter diary and portraits of J.B. – am answering shortly and have already begun the letter, but am sending you this first so you can get it off your hands immediately. No photos have pleased me so much as these of our morning wash and breakfast beyond Berwick – I've put the lot in an album and they look well. Your sleeping in clothes idea is an excellent one which I have never tried. Why not invent a suit that will do for dinner and bed and breakfast – so much pleasanter changing clothes at leisure after breakfast, (no gong to worry you, of course, as Mother will tell you, it never used to worry me, but then I was a model of propriety, you ask her) and again before dinner.

I'm hoping to get a motor-cycle up here before long, but you've one up on motor driving, though I can probably beat you on a cinema and typewriter.

Richie: Glad you liked the buck heads, from my window today the Persian mountains have been so clear, a veritable no man's land, except for robbers, but great for sport I believe. Between here and there, some 60 miles, it's just as flat as a pancake. I hope your farming efforts will be successful.

Alf: I've commented on your letter inside ditto I.R.E's – Have I had that answer yet?

I.R.E. More letters needed badly, none from you for tons of years.

From Richie.

Lassintullich,
Kinloch Leven,
By Pitlochry[1].
27th August 1917.

Dear Family,

We will not say anything about the remarkably short time this missive has been at R.M.C. as it would probably be censored by I.S. You will find a diary attached containing the doings of the first week of the holiday. I had a wonderful time and knew nearly all the sergeants on the place and half the officers. By this means (strategy) it did not matter when I got riotous and wherever I went, almost, I heard a voice saying "Hullo Corporal"! Mostly from the ten members of the guard whom I lived with for 24 hours. 9am. Sunday – 9am. Monday. The major who took care of us three from Rugby has just become engaged, but you will hear all this in the diary.

Last term I shot a lot. Only twice when I could have shot I did not do so. Once, to play my only game of cricket and once, to go to Coventry with the Architectural section of our N.H.S., when I had a good time. I shot fairly badly at first, but got better gradually and made top score on both sides against Uppingham; 94 out of 105 and once, in a practice, made 102. I won another cup for shooting at 500 yards, but lost the other one. Our house was in the cock-house match at cricket although at the beginning we had no distinctions.

On the last Monday of term we had the N.R.A. sniping competition for Public Schools. We had to shoot in the pouring rain the whole time so did rather badly, but came out third by one point. If I stay next summer I shall be vice captain of the VIII. Of course we beat Marlborough at cricket although Jack[2] put it down to bad weather.

---

1 This is a curious address as Kinlochleven is on Loch Leven well to the north west of Rannoch Moor whereas Pitlochry is well to the east. Lassintullich lies on Dun Alistair Water at the foot of Schiehallion.
2 Cousin Jack was at Marlborough.

The corps was inspected by Gen Smith Davies who underwent the painful ordeal of hearing me blow on my tooter!!! I did not ask him to listen. Daddy and Mother and some other person, whom I rather forget. Perhaps you will remember if I say that she has legs like the billiard table?!! They were there for the weekend and inspection.

We have been ensconced (not nothing to do with a quadruped) here for a fortnight and, despite the weather, are enjoying ourselves. The fishing is excellent. We have already almost trebled our bag of trout over last time. Today Mr Sorby and Daddy caught two weighing nearly two pounds and Uncle C got one of 1 lb a week ago. He left today (not the fish of 1 lb) and left me and Pom handsomely set up (10/-) (Irene, please withdraw your remark). He has been at his best and his stories, which you will find in Pom's diaries, are worth reading although you want him to tell them, especially the one about ferrets and gravy.

29.8.1917. Today we had an unlucky drive in the woods. I got one rabbit, the whole bag, although we saw about three roe deer. Mr Sorby got one the other day. We are getting lovely fish, yesterday two of nearly two pounds.

<u>Leonard.</u> (Grandpa) No ghosts now. I have not got a right and left at grouse yet, only ducks. Pom has bagged your room with a right & left.

<u>Tommy.</u> The grouse have nearly got over their fright from your shooting. There is one wasp nest on the other side of the river, another in a hole up the burn and a huge hanging one in the fir wood. Pom has not been stung yet.

<u>Vic.</u> (I.S.) I have gained much pleasure in once more gazing at your extraordinary handwriting. The censoring is foolish. Guilty conscience.

<u>Pom.</u> I will make no remarks as I can make them to your face.

<u>Irene.</u> I hear that I may have to travel to school with you. Poor me!! You are at present a gay young person.

Much love to you all from,

Richard Elmhirst.

DIARY (Richard Elmhirst)   (Referred to in his letter of
                              27th August 1917)

Wednesday 1st August

Nice long rest in bed, zzzzzzzzzzzzzzzzzzzz, though rather disturbed by people departing. Rose at 8am and dressed (uniform) and had a large breakfast. Said goodbye to three men, two were still in bed (9am). Got all our traps together, two kit bags of clo and two of signalling material and two bicycles. Get off by taxi to station. Arrived Northampton in pouring rain. We, a man in our house and I, were met by Major Crump adjutant 1st No V.R. These hieroglyphics mean

1st Batt North Volunteers Regt. We went by motor to the Territorial Hall, left our traps and went to the station to fetch bicycles. Got quite wet through. Then to Midland station, tea and train to Kettering. I had been invited to stay with my friend M. Found a dog-cart waiting and secured our Bikes to it and set off in blinding rain to Loddington Hall, 5 miles off. A lovely place, Tudor style all oak panelling and skins of lions and tigers on the walls. We arrived about 3pm. We only had the clothes we stood up in, so with Miss Steele, who has an invalid father and two brothers fighting, we routed out some of their clothes and I looked quite smart. The clothes fitted to a T. We then had tea (extensive). Afterwards, as it was not raining, we went into the garden and the greenhouses where we had one or two nectarines. After dinner we had grab snap, but as usual, the lady of the party easily won. Slept like a top, electric light over my bed. During the evening I played billiards on a full size table.

Thursday 2nd August.

Woke too late to have a bath!! Poured most of the day. Helped to hang some bacon. Cleaned my bike and buttons. Long walk in the afternoon looking for badgers. Did not find any.

Friday 3rd August.

Did have a bath!! Pouring rain again nearly all day. Dog cart to Kettering again. Caught train with ½ minute to spare. Northampton 11am. Got puncture on way to Drill Hall, left it to be mended at a shop. Waited about at Drill Hall, met another Rugby man there. At 1pm we went off to lunch with Crump, often known as

Muffin. We had a good lunch. He paid. We went back and packed things on to motor transports going to the camp. I rode another bike and we arrived at camp at about 3pm. Quite fine again. We had our tent allotted so:

Colonel Willoughby   Major Crump   us   command

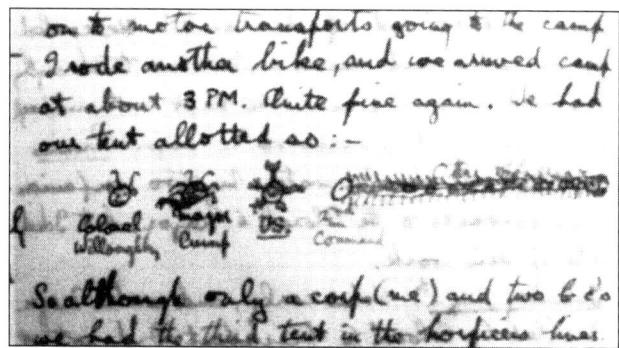

Images from Richie's letter of August 1917.

So although only a corp (me) and two Cc's, we had the third tent in the horficers lines. We went off to dinner then we paid ourselves. That night it rained hard and as no troop had arrived my friend and I were going guard, but Crump said I should have to go as guard bugler the next night so the other man whose name was Nisbet or Ears, who was very sick about being left in the cold, went instead. I slept fairly well. The second in command, Capt Birdsall, was dreadful for the first three days. He fagged us everywhere. He would come up and say "Oh you don't seem to have much to do. Get me some tent pegs and then some water to wash in." The only tap was the other end of the camp!! He cooled down later and never asked us to do anything. He was awfully nice. He kept meths and paraffin so I was able, by means of the Major's Primus stove, to boil shaving water. My two companions were servants to the Colonel and Major, but I did lots of their work.

Saturday 4th August.

Woke early and woke Major. Invited by Colonel to breakfast. Did not get any hardly. Forgot all us N.C.O.'s. This was our last private meal. Went to Northampton to fetch bicycle, also to order something for the Quarter-

Master (in private life a tailor). Got back and had a slack morning in my tent. At 1pm we went with our implements to snatch some food from the very mouths of about 30 men of the Labour Battalion who did odd jobs. They were a rough lot, but after a few days we used to crack jokes and josh them. We had roast beef and rice pudding. Then we waited for the arrival of the 1st Batt.

They arrived about 6pm. The Colonel, when they were drawn up, burbled for about half an hour on military law. Nobody heard anything until his horse got so sick of it, it got restless and the Major read all about penalties of death or any other such punishment which came every six weeks. We then went off to tea. At our table were two very nice men, one the clerk in the orderly room, the other a man who was in the Boer War. We had a real happy table always. I was in charge, though no one took any notice

Sunday 5th August.
Woke with Reveille, 5.30am. After breakfast I slacked about till I found that the guard had already fallen in, so I hurried into my equipment and dashed off. I was with the guard from 8am to 9am the next day. We did not do Church Parade as we were on duty. In the afternoon, instead of staying on duty, I went and talked to Crump, 2nd in Command, and had a nice afternoon. After all the evening calls, which went fairly well, I made my bed and went and dozed in the open. It was drizzling slightly, but I had a ground sheet over me. I knew the officer of the day would come and sure enough, at 10.45 he came around and we had to turn out to be inspected. Then I went to sleep in full equipment and was only woken by one of the guards shaking me. It was 5.15 so up I got and blew Reveille 10 minutes early, to the great sickness of the officers etc. I told them it was good for them to get up early. They had an early parade, 6.30 – 7.30. The guard had a nice hot breakfast, bacon and hot tea and tinned salmon. We started to be relieved at 9.00. The Colonel came along, very pompous and at last we were dismissed. I had my first good wash for three days. I did feel cold!! Then I went to M twice for letters etc. I visited the cook then. He showed me my lunch; roast beef, potatoes, plum duff. After lunch I went and congratulated him with the others. He gave us each a roast potato. We then marched off to some gardens where the Battalion

sports were held. They were rather dull except sack and obstacle races. I made the acquaintance of another sergeant who was bayonet instructor. We then trooped off to the Major who was sitting among all the ladies of the V.A.D. hospital. We went and joined them and were very gay. There was also a wounded Australian Officer I talked to. We got back at 7.30 and got turned out of the canteen, nearly, for our playful jests! There was a good sing-song which I did not attend.

Tuesday 7th August.

Did not wake with Reveille. I washed when I did wake, a record. I always washed in one of the officers tents. Capt Dadwell always told us never to throw water away except in the place provided, but we always managed to trip over a tent rope by mistake and we often saw him slyly emptying his. I went to M again, 1st to the G.P.O and Territorial H.Q. which was the other side of M and 2nd to take a telegram O.H.M.S. and to buy some chocolate for which the Major had given me 2/- to keep us three quiet. I returned him 1/- and some choc.

In the afternoon I learnt how to use a bayonet. Then a lecture on relieving trenches by the C.O. From 9 to 10.30 there was a firework display. Really it was some troops just ready for the front relieving trenches. They had gas helmets and tin hats. And there were mines and real gas and bombs, Verey lights and rockets. The noise was dreadful. Some of the V.T.C. collapsed. It was great sport. The Colonel came up and said, "did you see that, Crump?"

Wednesday 8th August.

Reveille blown so badly I was woken up. Route march, I was with the band. Afterwards, an inspection by the G.O.C. of the district with various red tabs. Afternoon, more bayonet fighting and I learn how to do an extended order, as if I had not done it for 3 years at Rugby! Good sing-song. I was asked to sing, but I had nothing to sing, though S students were there I believe. Pouring rain.

Thursday 9th August.

Woke only 1 hour after Reveille. In afternoon did Gun Hotchkiss I. Took it to bits. Visitors day. I took the V.A.D. Supt round. I lent her the

Major's gum boots. Night ops. I was orderly to Capt B. Quite a sport, relieving trenches. I dashed all round the place on my own nowhere near the Captain. Got to my dirty bed at 12 pm.

Friday 10th August.

Got up 1 hour before reveille. Packed up and said good-bye to the CO and my office friends. No time for breakfast. Took bicycle and kit bag to station for the 8.30 train. Had a pass.

From Alfred.   Elmhirst,
                                Barnsley.
                                23rd September 1917.

Dear Family,

As I write this epistle after a good Sunday lunch, sitting in the study, I perceive only a suspicion of a 'fusty smell' which a few of us may remember. We are nearing the end of a holiday in which much has happened. You will find my diary[1] enclosed gives a fair description of our doings in Scotland at Lassintullich, all except the journey down. Richie and I started off biking to Struan, while Daddy was going on the mail. We all arrived safely and duly got into the train and started off. At Ballinluig we saw the Aberfeldy Express!! We also saw Pitcastle and the thick wood and the wood above. We had some sandwiches and ginger beer at Perth. Then we started off again and got to Edinburgh in the afternoon. Then we went to the Station Hotel to get a bedroom, but the hotel was full up so we went on to the Waverley Hotel and got one bedroom there for all three. So we left our things there and then went for a stroll up Princes Street where we saw thousands of naval officers. In the evening we went to the Lyceum Theatre where we saw London Pride, which was very good. We got back about 10.pm and went to bed. In the morning we had a lovely hot bath!!! then breakfast. Our train was at ten so we started off (minus Mothers Burberry which was lost or stolen at the hotel). They weighed our luggage and found we had overweight, so we had to cart about 3 or 4 hundred cartridges about the station. We found we had two minutes to get the train and then we couldn't get a carriage. At last we found an engaged carriage, which we got into, with no-one inside. At York we had tea and when we got to Barnsley we found Vic and Irene waiting for us with the car. So we went home in style.

The next day was Sunday and on Monday we went to the baths with Alan Harvey. And in the evening Tommy arrived, so on Tuesday we went to Round-Green to get some partridges and went back for lunch. After lunch we looked over the car and replaced a sparking plug which

---

1   See Alfred Elmhirst's diary p. 159.

had given out. On Wednesday we went to Gainsboro' for some shooting, but did badly only getting two brace of partridges and two hares. We got very wet but got there and back quite safely. On Thursday we all went to the baths and had a lovely time. On Friday we went to Bitholmes[2], to try and get a bit of honey while Tommy drove Mother and A.F. to Miss Thorpe's. In the evening we had a bit of tennis.

On Saturday Tommy, Vic, R.E. and self all started off in the car for Howden to see over the aerodrome and call on Mrs Simpson. We got up to 50mph twice, but we were rather anxious about one of the tyres, so we did no more. We got inside the first sentry box when a tyre gave out and the petrol ran out. We put in a little more petrol and put on the spare wheel and went on. When we got to the garage we left the burst tyre to be mended and then went over all the airships except the Zepp for which we had to get leave. We saw Tommy's old ship C19 and his new one which was being built. Then we had lunch in the Mess and afterwards went over the Zepp. It was simply lovely and frightfully interesting. Then we filled the tank with 14 gallons of No1 Air petrol and put about 5 tins (10 gallons) inside !! Then we started off for Mrs Simpson, going through Laxton and Howden on the way. We had tea there and then started back. A few miles beyond Laxton we met a cart in a rather narrow place so went onto the grass at the side where there was a deep cart rut hidden by the grass. We got into this and it gave the front wheel rather a jerk getting out and suddenly, off came the right front wheel, and bounded along by our side as we went about 15 yards on the axle, tearing up the road. There we were stranded 2 miles from Howden and 50 from home. It was a beastly feeling, but it wasn't our fault so it was all right. Then Vic and I, leaving Richie in charge, walked into Howden and telephoned to Tommy and telegraphed home. Tommy sent his car and told us he would look after our car and get it to the aerodrome while his car would take us to the station to get a train at 6.40. We arrived home at 10pm rather tired. We don't know yet what's going to happen to the car.

---

2 Bitholmes, the tenanted farm near Stocksbridge.

I haven't said anything about school, but I have forgotten most of what I did, except that I just managed to get my 'flannels' for cricket. Irene's term starts on Tuesday. I go back on Wednesday, Richie and Vic on Thursday.

Leonard: There has been much disagreement about the famous sketch of 5th June waiting for Dr's rounds as to which is our lightning-artist. Could you enlighten us of the fact. We needed you badly at Lassintullich to double the bag!! Mrs Campbell wished to be remembered to you.

Tommy: I have just seen you and was listening on another receiver while you telephoned us at Howden P.O. after the accident. It is a nice car of yours, jolly comfortable. The driver was an awfully nice man. I hope you won the game of rugger.

Vic: Censor. He is far too efficient and has been un-necessarily careful about information to the enemy. I hope he will take notice of this 'note'. If the real Censor should happen to see this he will know it is not meant for him.

Richie: I think you put far too many sidelights on our correspondence.

Irene: I hope you will get on well with 'Old Fearsome' grim and gaunt. I hope she won't read your letters.

If anyone has the energy, time or temper to copy out my diary on foreign notepaper it would save our pockets!! Well it's time I stopped now so goodbye and good luck to all till we meet again.

Your loving brother Alfred. O. Elmhirst.

THE LASSINTULLICH DIARY   11th August 1917

Wake up in train at NEWCASTLE 4.am. VERY uncomfortable. MANAGE to survive to EDINBORO' where we change. Raining hard, get to FORTH BRIDGE. Tommy showed us the INDOMITABLE. (the FLEET was waiting below the bridge)

PERTH 9.am. where we got a minute breakfast. Waited a long time and at length reach BLAIR-ATHOLL. No car waiting for us as ordered so telegraph to Hotel, but that was a wash-out, so after a good lunch Richie and I start biking. They telegraph to PITLOCHRY for a car. Richie and I get to LASS all right, started tea and then came the others with all the luggage except the hamper (the most important thing!)

Daddy, Uncle C and Tommy go down to the river, get five fish, trout. I took rifle and got two rabbits.

Next day the 12th Sunday, go for a walk up the moor. In the evening T.W.E., R.E and self go on the river and take a big wasp's nest. Richie gets a sting, fine fun, take it back in a hanky! Late for dinner, but lots of grubs.

MONDAY. Start up moors, lots of showers, 18 brace grouse, 6 hares, 5 rabbits. After tea TWE, RE and self go to river again and take another wasp nest. No stings. Tommy got one in morning from nest in house.

A few good stories from Uncle C.

A gentleman arrives at Perth, asks a porter, "Where can I get tea?" The porter replies, "You've got te Perth."

Two boys out shooting with their respective fathers. First boy, "Look out Tom, you jolly nearly shot my guv'nor then." Second boy, "All right old man, don't mention it. Have a shot at mine."

TUESDAY. Pouring nearly all day so decide not to go on the moor, so T, R and self go to Loch Rannoch for day. Rotten sport only three small trout. Tommy goes in afternoon, motor to Blair Atholl (alone with lady driver!!) After tea we all went to the river for fishing (raining hard). Richie and I got nothing but four good rises, the other two got six nice trout out of the boat.

Some more good stories from Uncle Charlie.

A man got into a railway carriage, putting a basket tied up in a red handkerchief on the rack opposite to which he himself was sitting. After some time the man sitting beneath the basket suddenly puts his hand up to his neck and shouts to the owner, "Look out mister, gravy's running out of your pie." "Garn," says the owner, "that there's no pie, them's ferrets."

Donald Mackay and party, including an old keeper, coming to a steep stony hill when out shooting (the former being the only member wearing a kilt, all the rest wearing breeks) start sliding down. Donald, in great pain with all his skin rubbed off and clutching his kilt between his legs, is cheered by a remark from the keeper. "That's a nasty place for the kilt Mister Donald."

WEDNESDAY. Starts a lovely day. Go up to the moor, very hot, quite a good bag. 15 brace grouse, 6 hares, 1 rabbit and 1 Capper[1] which had been eating fruit in the garden. Just as we got inside it started pouring with rain and went on until after dinner.

THURSDAY. Rained all morning. Daddy and Uncle Charlie went fishing on Loch Rannoch. Richie and I fished the river, very strong wind, each party got four fish of a respectable size. No shooting.

FRIDAY. Started raining hard, but cleared up at 10.30. Sun out so off for a shoot through the meadows and a drive through a fir wood for roe deer. Very good sport and a fine mixed bag. 3 brace grouse, 1 brown hare, 2 snipe, 7 trout and 2 duck. "The meadows are of duck bereft, because of Richie's right and left." Richie and Leach got a brace of grouse! In the afternoon we all fished. Result: 7 fish. Tomorrow is booked up for the moor and it is my turn to shoot! Hooray!

---

1 Capercaille – a large game bird.

SATURDAY. Pouring rain all morning, so no going up on moor. After lunch we decide to do the woods above the house and part of the meadows. We start with the woods on the right of the house on the chance of some roe deer or some rabbits. We sight the roe deer which runs into the wood across the corn field so back we go and drive the wood up again with Daddy, Richie and Uncle Charlie posted along the top. Richie gets first shot, but misses it, then it turns and runs down the field in front of Uncle Charlie, who was out of shot, straight for Daddy who was behind a tree. He has both barrels at 20 yards, which appears to take no effect, so we (the beaters) start off to drive up the woods by the kitchen garden when Daddy shouts that he has found it. There it was in a hollow where a burn runs. The rabbits wouldn't be driven and there weren't many of them so it wasn't much of a success. Soon after this we saw another roe at which Daddy had a long shot, but without effect. It went quite close to Uncle C. but it was invisible to him so away it went. We got 12 rabbits which gave us some good fun, then in the meadow we got 4 duck.

From Tommy.   R. N. Air Station,
                               Howden,
                               Nov. 13th 1917.

Dear Family,

I am afraid I have kept F.B. longer than usual, but have been so very busy and besides which I can never raise any news, so always have delayed it a bit hoping that something might turn up. Nothing special has so I have at last decided to write and hope it will reach LKE for Christmas. I have just got my new ship flying, it did its first flight yesterday afternoon, great excitement, but quite successful. I can't enclose a photo of it yet, but might manage one, next time this comes round.

Tommy's airship P51 at Howden, East Yorks.
On patrol he said that he could pick up a submarine periscope at 400 yards but they could see his airship 2 miles away.

I smashed up my small car properly a fortnight ago, skidding backwards into a telegraph post about 30 miles per hour, luckily the three of us in it were not hurt, but the car looked a bit of a wreck and needs a new body, besides a few other little things, such as wheels, mud guards, axles, footboards etc. The old tub is still here, but I have heard today that the hub I have been waiting for has left the makers so I expect I shall take it home within a week. To V. R. and A, the back tyre, which looked in such a bad way on our run to Kexby and over here, went the other day when I was trying the car, and it took two men 15 minutes with a big blacksmiths hammer to get the wheel off. It had so rusted on, never having been off for about two years.

I have been playing a lot of Rugger lately seven matches in the last six weeks. We have only lost two, one against Ampleforth college, they played so fast that we were all tired out after the first ten minutes, so they won rather easily. We have come to the conclusion we shall have to go into training again before we play them next time, a little less smoking and drinking and late nights. The only other team that beat us was picked from 40,000 soldiers at Ripon. As we have only 18 here who play Rugger and it was our first game it was only to be expected.

I have managed to get in some good days shooting round here and also some good dances in York, so am having quite a gay time, but it is not all an easy time. The other day I went up and after being up a few hours, got caught in a gale of wind out at sea and only just managed to get back. At one time I had given up all hope out at sea of ever getting back to the land but eventually I found the coast after dark, found out where I was and got back here landing after twelve hours up on the last pint of petrol. Quite an exciting experience.

L.K.E. There is another book by the same fellow as Naval Occasions, just out, I will send it out if I can get hold of a copy.

Best of luck and affection to all from T.W.E.

From Leonard.   The Jumna Farm,
                                 Allahabad.
                                 Feb. 26 1918.

Dear Family,

Here endeth another chapter in the history of the F.B. for this is the last time it will have to travel out to India. By this day next month I hope to be on the briny once more homeward bound, and the very writing of the words makes me feel half there already. F.B. in fact should arrive one mail boat ahead of me.

I was staying down near Poona less than a week ago, and did not expect to be back North again till today when I received a letter saying that the Allahabad tribunal would hear my case on the 23rd, so off I came, a day in Bombay & then a 30 hours journey with a horrible night in a waiting room, stuffed with fleas, humming with mosquitoes, & certainly waterless. The farm is four miles out so I made for the cousin's house. You are all unfortunate in not as yet having been introduced to that branch of the family, however next time they are home I hope the fault will be remedied. They were only a mile away, & there is always breakfast, a hot bath & a welcome waiting.

Directly I had finished, it was time to approach the Tribunal. I'd just a notion that they'd be a bit stuffy, but they only asked one question & that was "for what date have you fixed your passage home?" – I said "that depends on you" they said "oh no, we only want to make certain you'd be out of the country by a certain date". So they gave me "total exemption". My passage is booked & my passport merely awaits the signature of some big-wig or other.

Meanwhile I have nearly another month before sailing, so I'm leaving the farm here with many regrets & sad leave takings, going to Bombay, collecting kit from various friends & agencies, rushing off another 900 miles to Madras round by Bangalore & Poona & back to Bombay in time for the boat.

It's a case of a bird in the hand & many people to be seen & said goodbye to in a very short space of time. So far I seem to have stuffed this letter with uninteresting details. Much has happened since June 6. when I wrote. The hot weather came on, & a wind that singed one's eyelashes blew, men died of it at an uncomfortable rate, & I was never so well for a long time. Just as the thermometer began to drop below 120 in the shade, I dropped with it, & after two days they put me on a stretcher, & via a motor launch onto a river barge with some fifteen officers & 2-300 men, we lay on the stretchers until the following day when they tucked us into bed down at Basrah, – the same ward I'd occupied on my first tour of hospital inspection. Then onto a liner & the first sumptuous meal for many months, but in a horrible atmosphere, & down to the Gulf where we went alongside a bigger liner still & were reshipped.

It was no voyage for an ordinary human, but it was in the right direction & we were treated royally, first class deck to about ½ a dozen sick officers and the same number of sick sisters. We were only able to appreciate our companions the last day or two. Then into a magnificent hospital in Bombay, where they didn't know the rules of the game & kept me three days too long. However I 'got clear' & shot off some 850 miles to Nanic Tal, & Emily Lodge where I had convalesced just a year before. The second day there I went for a walk with Lional Curtis of the Round Table, – (he acted as intermediary at the initiation of the Irish Convention being an independent politician who works outside the ordinary party politics area). For some time it was proposed that I should carry on with him. I'm glad I didn't now, though the month and a half was fascinating, – but by the end of it the convalescence had not begun to wear off, & so as we journeyed to Calcutta together he suggested my coming to this abode to recover on fresh milk, fruit, butter & air, – the superintendent being a great friend of his.

So here I've been ever since except for a little 2600 mile trip as Sec. to the boss, including 600 miles by motor through a Native State where the people are still slaves to all intents & purposes & the Maharajah runs his wives & other ladies, wears his jewels, & rides his elephants just like the 'Arabian Nights' princes. I have just been staying as his guest in his guest house, his father's palace, which was done up for the King's return when he visited the state.

From there I went to Bombay, working the typewriter, composing letters & seeing much of interest, thence to a meeting of the leading Agricultural Ministers & representatives, scientists, entomologists & economic botanists, & so leaving my boss. To Ahmadnagar, 600 miles to Madras, four days there, – a beautiful place in winter, you don't need blankets at all, all the year round, but Christmas is just pleasantly cool, – I saw all the sights there, chief among them being the Bishop's wife who is well known throughout India, – & so on up to Calcutta and back here for Christmas escorting two ladies all the way from Madras.

Just lately I've pulled off another trip arranged for me by Dr. Michael Sadler[1] a very different man from the brother we all know, no stutter, – into the wilds of the Deccan where the fighting chahratts live. I had five strenuous days there. We motored out to a little bungalow 36 miles from a railway & visited a village each day. I got a sketch of an old villager, who had grown the prize crop of potatoes & who on being asked his age said, he thought 50 but it might only be 30, & possibly forty years. – He looked ninety.

I can't tell you my exact date of arrival, but I'm sending this to Irene first, out of all order, because I know she should be at home away from the "Fearsome" clutches. I'll wire my exact date of arrival from London. Unfortunately I'm certain to be held up by the military there for examination & classification, but it means that directly the ordeals are over I shall be given leave to visit home. Departmental messages will have to wait till then for I'm in the middle of packing & am due to start at 11.0 tomorrow on a day and a half journey to Bombay.

To <u>Irene</u> – such a good letter arrived with three of Mothers' yesterday, dated 27th Dec & 3rd & 10th of January.

Please <u>all</u> manage to be home when I arrive. Yr affectionate brother Leonard

---

1 A Barnsley friend of Leonard and the family, he was also a benefactor of the Cooper Art Gallery at Barnsley and Vice-Chancellor of Leeds University.

From Richie. C/o C.E.M. Hawkesworth,
Rugby
22nd May 1918

Dear Family,

As someone else remarks, here ends another chapter of the F.B's existence. Next time it comes to me it will probably be at home or at Bushey, the Guards Cadet School. I got hold of a man from there on Sunday and got necessary particulars. I have to see my Colonel in town first. I shall spend the day there. Another day will be spent at Leamington being examined by a doctor. I am all aglow. Since last Sunday week we have been boiled alive. It has been lovely, but too hot to do much except glow.

As most of you know, I arrived back here on April 31st [sic] with huge box AND bicycle which was in a state of disrepair. I soon settled down, being in the same form and Stinks set, but having gone up another maths set to an old friend of mine who had me four terms before, he is a senior master called 'Moke' his name being Donkin. On the next Monday, being a day of distinction, I received five or six letters; one from the Aunts containing a generous sum which (perhaps you know) had been well hinted at.

I have shot four times this term so far, one time making 100 out of 105, but in a match on Saturday I only made 89 partly owing to a 'dud' cartridge, which lost me five points. At any rate I beat the captain. He may be leaving at the end of June leaving me to captain the XIII, that is, if I get my XIII first. We are going to have a match on Saturday after which I hope to get my XIII again. On Wednesday last we had a short field day not far from Northampton. It was quite good sport and we had tea provided. I met some lady friends from Northampton. They had brought with them some Girl Guides. I was introduced to one. We got back at 6pm with just time for tea and afterwards we had a topping concert by Miss M. Hayward and Mr Plunket Greene. He was awfully good, although a little passé. He was at his best 20 years ago. He sings most of his songs at about 120 mph and you can hear nearly every word. He sang 'Ethiopia' and 'A Good Old Irish Gentleman', same tune as our version, but words to correspond to a whisky drinking penniless Patrick, not a Sinn Feiner!

I have been farming twice this term. The first time it was a good way away, but what does that matter when you have a new back tyre costing a fortune of money. However it did matter, the front tyre could not stand it so rolled up flat and the front rim got its turn for a good few miles especially as I got the wrong road. The bicycle has now two fine tyres and two rotten mudguards.

The farming was nice and slack. We sat in some straw and had spuds brought to us to cut up for seed. We bandied words with some soldiers wives in a shed and a few Hun prisoners who kept driving past and who were quite jovial although they did not know much English. There are about 30 of them about here. They run quite wild except at night when they are cooped up. I also went farming today; in the morning we spudded thistles in wheat and in the afternoon we planted spuds, dreadfully hot, but not too strenuous. We are going to do the same tomorrow.

That's all my news and it is not long till we shall most of us see each other, though I may only have a week's holiday.

Your loving brother Richard Elmhirst. P.S. Alfie, this will do instead of a letter to you, but you had better write to me because you owe me 2/6.

From Alfred. Chernocke House,
Winchester.
May 1918.

Dear old 'Beans'! [new R.A.F. expression]

F.B. arrived especially welcome as I was in bed with some sort of disease which 9 other men got. No one can find out what caused it. Nothing very exciting has happened since I last wrote. Last term went off very well, I played many good games of soccer and scored quite a few goals.

We had quite a lot of diseases so raised four instead of three weeks holiday. This time I believe we are going to have 16 weeks !! i.e. till Aug 13th and then three weeks agricultural camp, but nothing is absolutely certain, though I believe the camp is going to be on Anglesey, so if I go I may be able to bike over and see Tommy occasionally.

I have had four quite good games of cricket, my average being 11. I should have played today only the doctor won't let me change. We got an extra half holiday today in honour of General Carey who saved the line when it had been broken in the Germans attack, by rushing up every spare man he could find. He was an old Wykehamist.

I think you will all agree that the censor[1] is making himself ridiculous by his superfluous little side notes although I will say that I show a great deal of decency and insight about it, as he says!!

I have just come in from playing cricket and had a rotten game as we had to field from 2 o'clock to 5.30 with no interval and then only had 25 minutes to make 278 runs in. At present we have only made 21 for 2, but we shall have to go on tomorrow, another man and myself are in. We also had a parade this morning and did coy drill, which was very boring. I find there is very little to say here as most of us met three weeks ago.

I had a very nice time in town with Leonard and the 'Psalmist' where he took me to tea and then to hear some gramophone records which he

---

1 Vic was inclined to edit his brothers' letters and thus became known as the censor.

wanted to try. Then we wandered about and I tried to get an extra hour or two with them, but could not manage it. Then we left the 'Psaltery', sackbut and all kind of music and Leonard and I tried to get a bus to Waterloo. In the end we walked there and got there at last. I got a ticket and a platform ditto for Leonard and found my luggage. Then we both sallied forth onto the platform where I met numerous friends whom I introduced Leonard to. Then we strolled up and down the platform until the train went off and in about two hours I arrived at my destination. And now I must stop and do some Homer and Heat. Now I can't think of anything more to say, so I had better finish up.

<u>Leonard</u>: I hope you have got some of those rockeries into shape at Elmhirst, which we so generously left for you. I have just had a letter from you, which I hope I shall have answered before you get this.

<u>Tommy</u>: You never got over to see me last holidays so mind you get over next, for a good long time. Your coaching on the tennis lawn at Pindar Oaks has done me a lot of good I'm sure. I hope none of your 'buses' have crashed lately.

<u>Vic</u>: You are an arrogant specimen of humanity. I wonder how you will change those words round. At present you seem to be having nothing but a slack time. I hope you will get some nice bathing.

<u>Richie</u>: You say I owe you 2/6d. I don't believe it. Anyhow you had better write and tell me what for. How is my friend Robson-Scott?

<u>Irene</u>: Have you heard the terrible news, that Don[1] has been run over by a tram and the workmen brought his collar to Uncle Charles and told him they had buried the remains. Thank you very much for your letter. I will answer it later, but I enclose a tie for you now.

Love to all, your loving brother,

Alfred. O. Elmhirst.

---

1 Don was Uncle Charlie's dog.

From Irene Rachel.   The Manor House,
                                      Brackley,
                                      Northants.
                                      2nd June 1918.

Dear Family, I received F.B. the other day with great delight; you bet. A good lot has happened since it last came my way. We are now sweating away at tennis and cricket, both great fun. Yesterday I played 4 sets in the afternoon and the temperature was about 75 in the shade!! The other day we had a cricket match and our side got the other side out in 2 overs and none of them made a run, then we went in and made about 17 in quarter of an hour and we have not finished it yet. Rather fun.

I have been put in charge of the cricket pitch and have to mow and roll it three times a week. I have three people under me. Of course, I order them about and they obey me!! The other day we went into another field near the playing field where there were some goats, an old thing with huge horns and two young ones. I and another went up with tempting pieces of grass and she looked quite amiable and the young ones jumping round. Then suddenly, just as we turned our backs she rushed at me and gave me a ripping butt, my word, she quite hurt. I then got hold of her horns and gave her a bit of a shake, not that it acted very well, still I had to teach her manners.

Irene Rachel with her school friends. (or perhaps the cricket pitch work gang?)

All the others were laughing. I wish they had got butted. Now I have got two un- named rabbits to look after. Old F[2] gave them into my charge with much ceremony, silly old thing she is. It's lovely having some farmyard produce to look after again, they are wild ones and quite tiny. I am afraid they will be eaten soon because this morning I said we should have to give them names. Old F chimed in and said <u>no</u>, they must not have names, because when we were eating them everyone would be saying that this one was Peter and that one was James; what bosh. What's the good of an animal without a name? She suggested at lunch today giving them some rhubarb pudding. I said I was sure it would give them a pain. A lot she knows about farmyard produce.

It's rather fun, we have all our meals outside now, useful for food disappearing under the table!!

I and one of the others (a Whitelocke) were invited out to tennis the other day. We had awful fun, of course the tea was the best part, but we had very good sets. We had lemon squash and ginger beer. I think that must have been given to make us play badly; certainly it is hard to play strenuous games on ginger beer, still everyone was the same!!

The play is coming off on June 24th. Great affair. I am sure I shall laugh just when I'm in the middle of a non-laughing piece. Also there is Speech Day when all the Big Wigs of the Woodward Community come down here and rattle off long dull speeches and crack up old F. She likes having the butter put on. Then there is the dancing display when we have three different costumes; one is old court ladies and jesters and in one of the others we are dressed up as wood nymphs with bare feet. My goodness we shall look funny. I know you will all make rude remarks about that. I can't remember the other dress.

Our form rooms get like fug-holes now with about ten people in and sun coming right in and one window that opens. People nearly faint. We have to go about twice a week biking round marking in things on ordnance maps, awful fag – still, the biking is rather fun. We biked one

---

2 Old F or Old Fearsome was Irene Rachel's headmistress.

Saturday afternoon to Banbury (10 miles) Altogether we went 21, quite good. We had tea and bought sweets there when the mistress was in a shop and then got well ahead going back and ate them, lovely.

We have not had any bust-ups yet, but I expect there will be one before long though because the hot weather seems to get on old F's nerves or something. Anyway the last week she has been very ratty, so something will have to be done, only everyone is rather too scared of her to do much!! Worse luck.

Well, I think that's about all the news that's worth telling. Oh, a boys preparatory school has taken a big place just down the road and Miss P. is getting in with the head and his wife. Their second XI wants to play us at cricket?? Mr. Broughton, he is the vicar you know who coaches us in cricket and, as I have once done a little over-hand, he is coaching me in it and no one else at present does it.

<u>Leonard</u>: Don't forget that you promised to take me up when you are in town. Also <u>don't </u>forget, that Brilliantine I gave you, I have just forked out 7/6 for a <u>tyre</u> so it will help!! Hope you aren't <u>tired</u> of <u>tiring</u> to read this <u>tireing</u> epistle. Good pun.

<u>Tommy</u>: Many thanks for a letter got yesterday. I do want to see the school photos back to see the remarks!! You might send one of the photos of you along with it.

<u>Vic</u>: Nothing to say to you as I only wrote to you a while ago, only just you mind how you censor this letter and let me know when you are made a Colonel!! Or anything higher.

<u>Richie</u>: Mind you make an effort to be captain of the shooting VIII. Does your study look as nice as when I saw it?

<u>Pom</u>: I hope you are not making it up about Don Tom. How awful, I am afraid I can't send a wreath to his funeral because he has had it and Uncle C. may not have him under a favourite apple tree in his garden!!!

Lots of love to everyone from your loving sister, Irene.R.Elmhirst.

From Leonard.   Pte. L.K.E. 768273
                                 C.ccy. No.11 Hut.
                                 2nd. Artists Rifles O.T.C.
                                 Hare Hall Camp.
                                 Romford
                                 Essex.
                                 England
                                 July. 16. 1918.

Dear Grandchildren,

Some of this letter must be to Pom, – for it was a great day in the annals of the family, & we were all grieved at his absence – twice, nay thrice I contemplated a telegram to his housemaster, but it would not have been worthwhile, – besides he is the only member of the family with any reputation left. By the way, coming down from Rugby yesterday, (yes, I caught the train, & had a good breakfast too, – please note IRE & JV) I happened on a letter, – on Brackley platform I think, & in trying to find out the owner I thought I recognised the handwriting, so between there & London I took a rough copy. Its hard to read I admit, but I gather it relates to the Saturday previous & was written by the headmistress, Miss Bridget (I think) Pearson to sister Belinda. I am not in the habit of reading other folks letters, but this seemed to have a family interest.

I like the idea of her "tickling the Provost's dainty palate" don't you, & also Miss S's "courageous intervention". It was "some stunt", wasn't it, – the first starter I gather was Vic (in bedroom slippers), "arrived at Nottingham". He gazed out of the window hoping to spot a well turned out Pte of the line, only to find himself confronted by the red tabs of a rosy cheeked staff officer, (sackbut, dulcimer & all kinds of music, complete) & by his side a pale stringy youth, smartly dressed in one of those "man about town" suits, made to fit you know.

I find now that the said brother, on discovery by an M.P., would have been sent out to France within three weeks – that's only a bit of wind however[1]. My next most vivid memory, is that of Vic & the said brother,

---

1 See Vic's biography for the reputed event.

shaking in their shoes outside the iron studded doors whilst locks bolts & bars were being dealt with on the inner side, being ushered into the giant's (ess's) den & sitting on the edge of their chairs being fixed with a stony stare by the said giantess[2].

Of a sudden, there sounded without, a fairy footstep, followed by a tender knock on the door, a slight shuffling followed by another little tap, – "come in" said the giantess (I suppose ogress, however appropriate, would not be polite). A knocking of knees & then with a cry of joy the princess fell into her lovers arms, – no <u>not quite</u>, she hustled the two princes into the passage, gave the door in front a lusty kick with her dainty foot & almost fainted with surprise & delight. (That's good, but I can't keep it up in spite of a day's not duty.) I can leave the peach episode to Vic, the raspberries to Richie, the flag flying to Tommy, – altogether it was a most successful day, even if three budding Eve's did lead us astray. Of course the Adam's took all the blame & left the garden. – There was a great fluttering in the dovecot, – but I've already forgotten the names of those young damsels to whom I was introduced. Miss Constance Marriott, I think I should remember anywhere.

The Psalter met me in town, with his Papa, who is a dear old man, & we walked to Papa's club, left him tottering up the steps & then turned down to Whitehall. Great fun, I only saluted gold braid & passed all other stars & stripes without a nod, – merely fixing them with a stony stare.

We attended the zoo in the afternoon & discussed the disadvantages of matrimony at some length, if I remember right, (it's all right there aren't many but there are some).

Meanwhile I must say farewell.

Yr. affec. grpa.

Leonard

---

[2] This seems to have been an encounter with Rachel's headmistress, Old Fearsome.

From Vic.   A. Coy. R.M.C.
                                        Camberley
                                        Romford
                                        July 28 Saturday 1918

Dear Family

I will make an effort to be good, but it will have to be a great one after what I have read about your Humble. <u>It</u> reached me when I was seated in our Ante-room with my pop-gun and puttees waiting for our parade and, being far too bulky to disfigure my pockets, was left on the table there. I will now start a little resume (?spelling) of my past deeds starting the day I went to town.

As I had to report at the R.M.C.[1] between 3 and 4 pm I was compelled to start the day before and spend a night in town.

That day I was to take Daddy and my luggage to Cudworth in tub, come back and go by velocipeed to my train later. I set off with car and arrived <u>just</u> in time, but coming back, just as I was getting up to 40 in the place where Irene knows, the health and life giving substance gave out and we came to a full stop. As I had to get home and then to Cudworth in the next hour or two I felt weak in the fins but pulling my bits together and leaving the other bits in charge of an old man hacking up the road, I started home (not at 1 mile pace as heat was more than half what Leonard gets). Just before reaching the Viaduct, a lorry met me and I asked if they had a tin to spare. Theirs was all in the tank but they told me a shop fairly close where I might get some. With many thanks I pursued my way to the shop which was between the Viaduct & Canal, at first he was unwilling but with gentle voice I gradually persuaded him and he began to walk slowly to his motor shed (I was in an excrutiating hurry but did not dare to hurry him for fear of annoying him). At last I <u>got it</u>, giving him 7/6 to be returned if I brought him another tin. On my way back with 2 gall tin a tea tray passed me and kindly gave me a lift like this.

---

1   Royal Military College, Sandhurst.

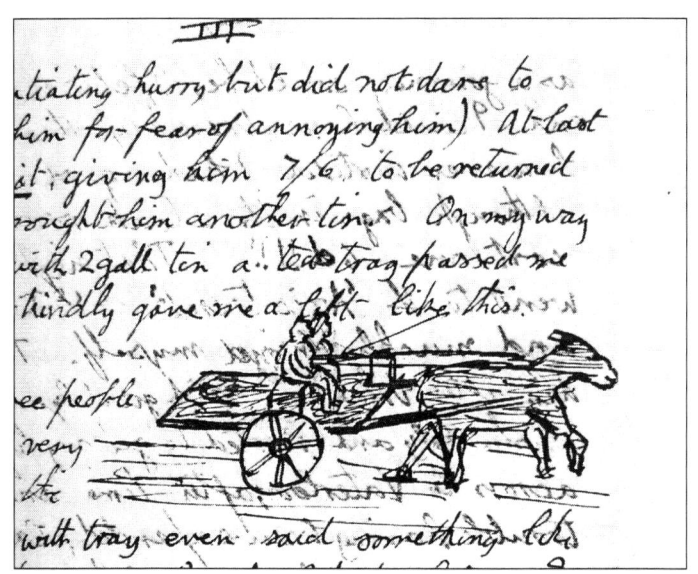

The horse and cart drawing referred to in Vic's letter of 28th July 1918.

All three people were very nice, the last one with tray even said something like 'Don't mention it' when I thanked him. I got home at last and started off almost at once on my bike to Cudworth + tin, one (1), petrol for the use off, full. I found I had mislaid my Health Certificates so Alfie went back to try and find it while I went on to Cudworth. As the train came in, Alfie arrived somewhat warm minus Cert<u>e</u>, One, Health. We then wept a farewell and I set off. Of course forgetting a bike ticket. The journey was hot as a journey could be, I felt at the end I could have drunk up the sea, however instead I had a good tea although bags in the cloakroom cost me 6d!!!!

That night I went to the 'Aristocrat' at St. James and muchly enjoyed myself. The next day after breakfast I said goodbye to Cousin Lily and started to get my luggage across to Waterloo, after time and trouble being expended, Caesar succeeded in embarquing with all his baggage and advanced to meet the unknown barbarians.

Halfway there I met three Marlborough chaps (men if you like, Alfie) so felt much better. About 10 people were coming by that train and there were 3 cars waiting but the baggage was packed on them while the personnel biked (L.K.E. did you know my bike has taken a new lease of life). The Grounds are lovely consisting of fir woods chiefly, which have a priceless smell in this heat; three large lakes, two used for boating, the other for swimming; an expanse of grass for games and also a large amount gravel surface for drill. If you get all the sense out of this you will have done well.

After waiting in front of "A" Coy block for some-time, our future staff-sergeant took us in, showed us our rooms and after reporting to our Coy Com<u>dr</u> we began to settle down. The next day we were issued with books and equipment and tried on for clothing and boots. We now began our 6 weeks squad drill on the square, a fearsome business especially with a pair of GS boots (General Service) with 99 nails in each boot.

There was another Marlborough chap in A Coy and on Saturday we got a pass and went to Farnborough to try and find the aeroplane sheds. We failed so came back and boated on the lake.

I am now tired of writing as it is 3.30 and I started looking at FB at 12.15. Now to resume as Alfie says. I read till 4.30 then had tea and bathed from about 5.30 to 6.30 or 7, change for mess at 8 and began again at 9 pm clad in white shirt and black trous. Quite early on I had invitations from Mrs Chignell and Mrs Cairnes, some of Mother's friends, and they have given me a lovely time. As a matter of fact I have been to tennis at Ascot to Mrs Cairnes and her friends nearly every Wednesday and Saturday except about six times in the last nine weeks bringing a friend or two every time. Imagine my fright the first time we went when we found 9 ladies there but only one other man. The ladies were very nice however though some are much too good at tennis for the likes of me. They all seem to be working at the hospitals and canteens round here but now several, including Mrs and <u>Miss Cairnes,</u> have let their houses and gone away for a month or more so I am having some peaceful Saturdays etc. You see we had to bike 9 miles there, play tennis really hard as there were not enough gentlemen and then bike back at a furious speed as they always kept us at the tennis too late. We do that 9 miles in about ¾ of an hour nearly every time, though once I got a puncture near Ascot and did about 6 miles on the rim of my 'puir ould grid'. However she is a stout old thing, quite worthy of me as she only raised the one puncture which sent her flat; she also has no three speed wire and every time to Ascot my legs have twinkled round on low gear.

In the sports I was running for 'A' Coy in the mile with four others, but after getting through the first round first out of the four others, I arrived about 3 secs late in the second round as they ran the 4th heat 2nd so I was chucked out. The following is the programme for us juniors.

First 6 weeks	Squad Drill
Second 8 ---	Musketry
Third 4 ---	Company Drill
Fourth 1 ---	Field Training
Fifth 1 ---	Battalion Training
Sixth 2 ---	<u>Recess</u>, Leave, Holiday, Vacant
	[No scribbling here please JVE]

The first ended up with a Drill Competition in which we unluckily came in 8th out of 12 as we 'got our wind up', stage Fright, etc. In Musketry we did better getting 2nd making the best average score on record at 30 out of 45 at practice: 'The Mad minute' where you load and fire 15 rounds in the minute at a 4 foot target at 399 yards. The Course is great sport and I raised marksman's points so was very pleased!!

Company Drill we do with the Adj: a splendid fellow. He did awfully well at Antwerp but a derrick fell on him and caused the loss of one eye and smashed his leg to bits. You could not tell this however as he is by far the smartest man here (His name is Dalrymple-Hamilton)[2].

Field Training. Well it <u>is</u> training!! Company attacks wearing full marching order ie Web belt, pouches, bayonette, entrenching tool, water bottle, haversack and pack, the latter containing about half a years clothing and room. Battalion Training is the same only with Batt<u>n</u> and consequently a few degrees worse.

---

[2] By an interesting coincidence, when the writer's son, Maj.C.M.Elmhirst, was the Sandhurst Academy Adjutant, O.Cadet E.Dalrymple-Hamilton (the great nephew of the above mentioned) was one of his cadets.

With all this we also have P.T. (Physical Training), Trench Digging, and lectures on Military Law, Organisation Tactics, Trench Warfare, Map reading and Field sketching. Despite all these I enjoy myself thoroughly and perspire freely. Just now, at the end of the third period we have been drilling like mad with colossal tons of inspections for the King's arrival & inspection tomorrow.

Yesterday and today the match between RMA[3] & RMC has been played, but I'm sorry to say we lost by 6 wickets though we won on the first innings. A few weeks ago a friend and I helped to pull down a balloon with one passenger like Tommy used to have. He had come through a storm and was soaked to the skin. We helped to pack the thing up and get it off. It is now 10.30 so I had better stop and get to bed as lights go out at 10.45.

After rumours lasting about two months the King[4] has at last been to inspect us, bringing as well the Queen and Princess Mary. The Battalion did really well I believe so that everyone from the King downwards was frightfully bucked, also you really should have heard the send off he got; his car could only go very slowly as there was a large crowd of GC's all round, some even hanging on to the mudguards cheering for all they were worth; I got in the middle of the road so that when he came past I was in the front rank and had a real good view. They all looked immensely pleased, though the King looked awfully tired and worn out. I should not like to do all he has to do. We were very glad that in his speech he congratulated our Adjutant very highly as the latter is the making of us and is a great sportsman.

<u>Leonard.</u> Please excuse me for any insertions in your beautiful letter. I have managed this much better for once.

<u>Tommy.</u> I suppose you will have your new ship ready by the time this comes to you.

---

3   Royal Military Academy, Woolwich. The RMA and the RMC merged in 1947 to become the RMAS (Royal Military Academy, Sandhurst).
4   King George V.

<u>Richie</u>. I got a surprise the other day, found Paget at my Coy entrance asking for me. He is a Corporal, quite a knut.

<u>Alfie.</u> I found two envelopes in my drawer with this inscription.

Sugar		
Dog biscuits } Coop	Braces	Richie you will
Bells & Pipes Rushforth	Sponge bag	remember this
Potatoes	Cider	
Pain	Fertiliser!!!!	
Dentist		
Boots		

Irene last & least I expect you are riding Pink (?) Foal etc bare back now.

Yrs + Boots!!

Vic 1 Brother

From Richie.   Elmhirst
                                Barnsley
                                Aug 18 1918.

Dear Family,

I have only kept F.B. one fortnight and it is going quite a good pace, and except for Pom, we all saw each other at a certain spot in the Midlands a little time ago.

I did some rowing at Brid when I was there, and got two lovely blisters. A week after I got back I had lovely blood-pisining [sic] in my right palm, and this is the second letter I have written since, though Leonard's typewriter came in handy (A letter came this morning from Leonard saying that we could use his bicycle and his typewriter). I thought it would as I used them in advance. My hand was real 'fruity'. I had a very good term last term, which finished up with our winning the N.R.A. Sniping Competition, though Pom says Winchester would have won it if they had had all their men but we were the same, one man (top score) came out of the San that morning, another could only just last out to the end, and I got the flu an hour afterwards, and so we were eight points behind our record score.

We did not lose a single shooting match last term. After the expedition to Brackley, I did not do very much work but we had to sweat up for camp and Drill Camp and there were exams of which I did not do many, but managed to go and pick fruit with some others and talked to two nice young ladies.

Our house was 2nd in the Drill Camp, I was No I Section Comm.

The day after I had drawn my kit for camp at Wellbeck, the W.O. order came cancelling it. Practically everyone was glad and there was an uproar in the house, though everyone had been willing to go. I went and consoled the O.C. and said I had just accepted an offer to go and watch the Marlbro' match. A day or two after, he came and asked if it was too late to invite me to go with him. He is a sportsman.

On the last Sunday we had quite a good house supper because we were Cock-House cricket and the House Butler, who has been forced to join up, received a cheque for £30 odd collected in the house. I hope he won't drink it all!

Next morning I went across to Mr Martin's house and we set off up to town. We got there at 11 and went to the Bath Club and then took our luggage to Padders. We then went with Capt of the Rugby XI and had lunch at the Picc. Grill, and he left so late that he only just caught the Marlbro' train at 2 PM.

Then I went to see the Naval Pictures and Philip joined me later and I went round again. Most of the family have seen them now, they were good but there was a scrum.

We then went for a bathe to the Bath Club, and there decided to miss our 5.30 train, spend the night in London and go on the next day, especially as it was pouring. So by means of tubes we only went backwards once. We got our luggage and got to the York hotel. In the evening we went to see 'The Boy at the Adelphi' it was good. On the way back we bought <u>6</u> boxes of matches from an old man.

We had to get up at 6AM next day and arrived at Marlbro' in pouring rain to find both XI's playing billiards. So we joined in and walked up to the school buildings, but it was so wet we retreated again, had a good lunch and decided to come home.

So we started 3.30 and got home at 11 PM but were not expected till 11.30. (They played at Marlbro' next day. Two of our men could only just stand up and the captain was just recovering from flu and we were beaten by an innings, though they said there that we should beat them).

We had a most enjoyable week here, what with our midnight amblings and gardening, although Tommy and Philip mostly took it in turns to sleep on Leonard's sofa (Admiral's Barge).

On Tuesday, it was boiling and I had to go and meet the exception to the Fearsome rule at Penistone. There was one mistress, the one who talked to us and a whole bevy of young ladies who all tried to peep at me from behind the safety of Miss ---'s skirts!

Of course Irene came by the train with no connection at Penistone so, like Vic, we started off by road, although we each had a bike, but Irene's had a flat tyre.

We got home via Stainbro' at the last gasp but managed some food, Irene ate ravenously, of course, being starved at Brackley unless the fruit, especially raspberries and nectarines are in season.

The next day I went off with Philip to Brid. I had written to Uncle C[1] and we found him and he gave us a good lunch and took us round the museum. Then he went off and we went round the Minister together and then had some tea and left for Brid at 5PM. The train was pretty full and about 15 minutes late in starting. A man rolled up ten minutes late and as the lady ticket-collector remarked "If the train had gone you wouldn't have caught it", which was quite true though rather obvious.

We arrived at Brid about 8, rather fratchy to find that the landlady refused to take in 10 of us. But we did not see her till next morning and Philip calmed her down and we went to look for a room where two could sleep out.

Then we went to Mrs Harland's and she did not recognise me at first and was very proper but when she did she took me along to where Tom, Molly & Barber were. Then we went bathing leaving Mrs H and Philip who were going to look for rooms.

After a rather cold bathe, we met them. They had found a room close to ours for Mr and Mrs Martin and I was to stay with the Harlands.

They looked after me awfully well, though it was rather hard to be polite and refuse meals so that I could go with Philip and family which consisted of Mrs Martin, two children + nurses and three cousins.

---

1 Uncle Charles lived in York and was the secretary of the Yorkshire Philosophical Society based at the Yorkshire Museum.

We had a very good time, went for a row twice, too rough for fishing, nobody was sick. We often went on Princes Parade to see the type of Bridlington visitor though most of them were so hidden in paint, you couldn't see them. Our speciality was a walk, Mr, Mrs. & self at 9 PM along the sands when we got as far as we could. We paddled and came back at 10 PM. I always left about 10.15 for my 'lodgings' where we sat up a little longer and had cocoa. One night an American came in. He was rather dull and at quarter to twelve Mr H had to say we were going to bed or he was going to stay till the early hours I think.

I played tennis up at the club once, but the tournament I was to play in was put off. I left at 3.30 on the Monday and got home to find Miss Coleclough and Gerald here.

The fete was on Wednesday, quite a small affair after the one in 1915, but Houp-La made £3-5, and altogether Mother scraped together about £40.

Then my hand got bad, but we have been to two cornfields (one the old moleing field). I have had five shots and have got three rabbits. Conus worked quite well at R. Green in the corn but we only had two shots and got four rabbits. It is quite funny to see him bouncing about after a rabbit.

Irene & I go to Arkendale[2] and Elvington[3] tomorrow we hope. I go to Bushey about 6th Sept I believe for about six months.

Quite a long letter for me, and if they are too long they take up too much room and are not worth reading.

Your loving brother

Richard Elmhirst

Where's your letter Leonard? Is it the Brackley serial?

---

2 Arkendale, the home of his maternal grandparents.
3 Elvington, the home of uncle Herbert, father of Jack and Cecil.

From Alfred.

Elmhirst,
Barnsley.
1st October 1918.

Dear Family,

For the first time since the F.B. has been in my possession, I have kept it over a fortnight! Which is more than some of you can say!! Still, I had an excuse, as I couldn't answer it in a way seemly for F.B. at camp not having the proper utensils and only getting an hour of daylight to yourself the whole day.

It does seem funny now to get the F.B. twice a term instead of about once a year! I got on quite well last term and in the last order at the end of the term 8 men got removes into Senior part and I was 9th so missed it. But, I may get a long service one yet! I also managed to get my house tie for cricket and am now captain of the house XI. I also shot for the VIII and got the 2nd top score for the Pub. School. Sniping competition. 102 out of 105. Top score was 103. We only had a week to practice in.

They gave us 3 weeks extra term to be ready for the Anglesey harvest and when we got there we found that the farmers did not want us for a week or two. All the same, they made us sweat away 18 hours a day. But the second day, a friend and myself got leave to go to T.W.E. (Tommy) who we thought was about 4 miles off.[1] We started at 6.pm and had to be in by 9.pm. So we started off by losing our way, then we went miles round and then when we were nearly there, we went another 2 miles out of our way, then at 8.pm we got there. They were in the middle of dinner, but T.W.E. came out and took us in to mess and we sat down to dinner.

At 8.48 we went out to see the Airships. Everything was awfully interesting, we saw one land too. About 9.pm or after we thought it was time we were going back. Tommy was going to a dance at Bangor which

---

1 Tommy by this time was 22 and, as a Captain in the RNAS, was Commanding Officer of the Anglesey Airship Station. He was made an acting Major in the newly created RAF when the RNAS and the RFC (Royal Flying Corps) merged at about this time.

was along our way, so we left our bikes there and Tommy drove us into camp just as lights-out were going.

Slight sickness from the C.O. but cooled down a bit by Tommy. Next day was a half day off, Sat, so off I went again and spent the afternoon with him. Coming back late again, more sickness this time and says something will happen next time. I manage to get back just in time next day. Work the whole of the week then Saturday afternoon off to the Aerodrome. Tommy gone away, nobody knows where to or when he'll be back so another officer ups and asks me to go with him to some friends for tennis and tea, so off we go on bikes, neither of us knowing the way. We got there at last and had tea and played tennis. I played in a filthy shirt, khaki bags, black socks and a pair of old slippers they found. Still, no one minded. We overstayed our time again and had to race back. I had to go on in front as I was bugler and had to blow first post. I just got in in time although I went miles out of my way.

Next day I went to some more of his friends (all T.W.E's friends too) all awfully nice. We had tea and talked and just before we left they asked us to a dance the next night. We thought a letter from them to our C.O. might do it, but no luck, it was a pity. Still, they asked us for the next Sunday and the other people for the Saturday so we were fixed up. I came off my bike really well that week, so it put me out of action for a day or two. So, as I couldn't do corn work, I went to a garage to see if they could let me have a tractor job so they sent me off to a field where a Ford was towing a binder and I spent the whole day there. It was great fun. Next day I went to another tractor, then I drove a Titan about 6 miles along the roads to a farm and did these kind of jobs the rest of the time. Next Saturday I was just going off to my tractor when the Superintendent of tractors said "Would you like to see a bit of the Island with me?" I said "yes" and got into the Ford van, put my bike on the back and set off. We took some oil and paraffin round to a few tractors and then went round to find out farmers who wanted tractors. He wasn't a very good driver, this man, and went deadly slow so I said, would he let me drive.[2] He was a bit doubtful but said "all right." I started off not having the faintest idea

---

2 Pom was just 17, but this was in the days before driving licences.

of how a Ford car went, so at the first hill we stopped. I said something about just having forgotten how it went and then he showed me and off we went.

I took him at about 35 the whole way and round the corners, I saw him fair gripping the side, but I was very safe and got on quite well. At the end he said I was a very good driver! Then off with my bike and on to the Aerodrome. There I found that Tommy had to go to Holyhead on business so he lends me his little car and a driver to go to my tennis party in. Being in good driving form, I drive the whole way there. We had some good games of tennis, one set being 3 a side. The trouble was, since 4 officers hadn't turned up, as it was a flying day, I was the only specimen of my sex there and there were 5 ladies! Still, all went off well, though there were going to be prizes and a proper tournament.

I found I was an hour late in starting so hurried up and drove the whole way back. Then, at the Aerodrome, I found I had 10 minutes to get back in (8 miles) so put bike on Tommy's car and set off to camp and got there under ¼ hour driving myself the whole way. Next day friend and self set off to last Sunday's friends and got there very wet, but changed and had lunch, then we all set out to more of their friends for tea and quite by mistake I met Tommy and 2 other officers there so we all made a good party and had a good time.

They had to go early so we stayed on a bit. Then we left and this time got home in good time.

On Wednesday I set off to the station at 8.30 and got to Holyhead. There we waited for the mail boat from Ireland then went off at 12.pm and eventually got home at 8.30. The same evening Tommy arrived on leave for a few days and Vic and Irene at home too. They all went in time and the next week Irene and I set off to Coumes at 12.pm for blackberries. We took a long time to get there because of wind, but we got there and then had our lunch having picked one or two blackberries on the way up. Then we went up the wood and found - well, more than we could pick in a week - so we set to and by 7.pm we had got about 6 lbs. Then we started back and before we got to Birdwell we found it was after lighting up time so we had to go down Rockley[3] and it was pitch black under the trees. Still it was late and we had to get on so no brakes. We got back at 8.30 and had a bath and dinner to ourselves, such a good one, making up for lost time (and food).

Next morning we got woken up by A.F. at 5.am to go to a cub-hunt at Ackworth 10 miles away at 7.am, so at 6.am, off we went and got there in just an hour. (I have been having to tow Irene everywhere as her bike is such a fiddling little velocipeed.) We followed them on foot and bikes for about 12 miles, all but getting our bikes stolen into the bargain, but it was good fun.

We slept in the afternoon and had a good slack. A few days after, Irene went off to the Nunnery. I biked there in ¾ hour against an awful wind and got in just in time to see her get in with the "College Meadows". On Wednesday last I set off at 10.am with clothes in haversack and bike to Wakefield where I entrain to York, thence I bike to Elvington and stay with them until till Friday morning.

I caught the mole that had been damaging the whole lawn by my skilful wiles, then on Thursday I set off on my bike to York and called on Uncle C. who said I had better go around the Minster till 1.pm and then call for him. So I went over it and paid 6d and went to the top of the tower and got a good view. Then I came down and went over the part below and saw a tablet to Admiral Cradock. Then I met Uncle C. and went out to Terry's for lunch. Then we spent 2 hours in which he took me round the museum which was all very interesting. Then I went back to Elvington in nice time for tea.

Next morning I set off home biking all the way. No body there knew the way and I had forgotten the Michelin Map at the last moment so in time I found myself on the outskirts of Howden and I saw the airship sheds. So, back I went and got to Selby and in time, i.e. 3.15pm, I got home having started at 10.am! Next morning a tragedy occurred, who should turn up (or in as the case was through the larder window) but Vic! There

---

3   The back road from Birdwell to Round Green and then to Elmhirst passes through Rockley.

he was when I came down looking forward to my breakfast, it quite put me off it. I think only a very scratchy mapping pen could get remarks in there.

Leonard: Many grats on getting to Bushey. Write and tell me about it if you have time. Perhaps you will have demobilised before the year is out??!!

Tommy: Many thanks for all your help and everything in Anglesey. You say in your letter that anybody can have a photo. You did give me one in Anglesey, but I couldn't lug it away on my bike. I'd like an arm and a leg one signed if possible. You will be having another one taken in "brass hat and blue uniform" soon I expect.

Vic: This letter equals yours and beats it, try counting the letters.

Richie: It is the first time in my life (and yours) that we haven't seen each other in the holidays, (nice for me). Are your lady friends very nice?!

Irene: I hope as Head of School you are bringing up the standard of the school. I expect another Reformation is needed in the way of 5 brothers!!

Extract from I's letter. "We have another Irene in the school now, she is very nice too" Unintentional, but take note what omission of stops leads to! I could write more but I'll leave it to others.

Pots of love from your affectionate brother Alfred. O. Elmhirst

From Irene Rachel.   Elmhirst,
                                      Barnsley.
                                      11th January 1919.

Dear Family, I really think it's about time F.B. started once more on its journeys. It has been having a little rest cure with me. As all the family have been home for the hols there is not much fresh news, but Pom and I think that if I put a few of our happenings in the hols when we were all together as otherwise no one would remember.

We had a very good Xmas day when Uncle C dealt out his 10/-, he and the Aunts came for lunch. We also have raised a flag for the old summer house which Leonard, Vic, Richie and Pom <u>and</u> me put up the morning that they came home.

L.K.E., R.E and A.O.E. came at 6.30, Thursday Dec 19th. I was there to receive them having come a day earlier. Vic came at breakfast time. We sent the flag up and gave three rousing cheers! We all went down town to meet Daddy and Tommy who were coming from Goathland. And all, except Daddy and myself, who drove up, walked up from the town "baggy breeks" and all! We had many most exciting shooting days with rabbits getting 19 shots apiece before they turned their toes up etc. Then lunch with a good fug up with a nice hot fire in the little wooden hut, also an exciting drive home with Pindar dashing up perpendicular hills with five people, guns and game etc aboard, and the harness breaks, but all was well and all helps to keep up the spirits of the happy home! But they were good days shooting with everyone blazing away merrily with occasionally something to show for it.

Among other things we went to Aunty Min's[1] for dinner and games. Tommy was feeling indisposed with Xmas fare!! Of course everyone, except myself, ate and drank (drank especially) much too much, so after partaking of Bacchus's merry cordials, the gentlemen sang and acted seemingly with much alcoholic inspiration and by the "light of the silvery moo-oo-oo-oon" we rolled merrily home having had a most hilarious evening.

---

1 At Round Green.

By the way, Mr Lee said to Daddy today after church that he had told his wife, what a beautiful sight she had missed on Xmas day of the family in the pew!![2] Also during the hols we "souped" and cut logs and had a most exciting game of hockey on the lawn.

The great event of the hols was going to a play "Betty" at the Empire Palace to which Tommy gave us two Christmas boxes. It was topping, the boxes being each side of the stage so we could look across at each other and, of course, all the ladies on the stage went the other side and the gentlemen came our side! It was most thrilling, we created quite a sensation!!

After that everybody began to trickle off, Tommy starting on the Monday Dec 29th. Last Wednesday Leonard appeared at 11.30, and only succeeded in waking me by throwing snowballs at our windows. Conus got most excited, Leonard afterwards had some silly notion about me thinking it was burglars and putting my head under the bed-clothes, but that's just bosh he's made up. Anyway, I came down and let him in without rousing the house and, after talking a bit, bundles him off to bed with Pom who was asleep with no window open and curtains drawn. But Leonard soon remedied that.

Next morning Mother went in to their room, did not notice Leonard, and said to Pom "What a good boy, you are with window open etc, why, Leonard might be home again!!" and went out!! Leonard departed for Ireland next morning at 5o'clock. We all got up and had tea etc. I hope he had a good crossing.

We have been twice out shooting since; once to Ouslethwaite, where I picked up 8 snickles round one stick heap, but we got four rabbits. Then we went to R.G.[3] on Friday getting 7 rabbits, 1 pheasant, 1 waterhen, 1 stoat – which old Jack J bolted out of a rabbit hole on the boundary of Yew Tree hedge. He was a whopper and old J.J came out with tail all of a bristle! We brought him home to skin him, but he was shot too badly.

---

2   The old family box pew at St Mary's Church, Worsbrough.
3   Round Green.

<u>Leonard</u>: I hope you were not <u>very</u> sea sick and have got some nice work to do in your new abode. Good luck for the new chapter.

<u>Tommy</u>: I am very glad to hear you are getting another Barnsley Main. I hope you will get your coupe soon. Remember you are going to fetch me home in it.

<u>Vic</u>: You say some rude remarks in your letter, which is not unusual style. I suppose you can't help it so I will forgive you this time, mind you write to me <u>this</u> term.

<u>Dick</u>: I hope you are not very lonely without your elder brother, praps you'll get on better without him. (I hope he won't read this) How many ladies <u>did</u> you kiss at that party at the Bournes?!

<u>Pom</u>: Well, you are here at present so, instead of saying rude remarks, (most needful) I can impose them. You will take the consequences – tomorrow prps.

Good luck to everyone from your loving sister, Irene.R.Elmhirst.

From Tommy.   R.N.Airship Station,
                               Llangefri,
                               Anglesey.
                               7th March 1919.

Dear Family,

I am the culprit this time having kept F.B. for nearly two months, still it is the first offence! My news since the Christmas leave when we all met is not very much and I have since seen Vic at Holyhead, Richard at (1) Rugby, (2) Piccadilly Circus, (3) Watford and Irene at Brackley so most of it is known.

I have now put up the A.F.C. ribbon (red and white) which I think goes very well with the 1914 one, however I.R.E. says they don't go well together and I suppose she ought to know!! I have had thoughts on leaving here on more than one occasion, but nothing has come of it, so now expect to wait here until the station closes, quite probably about the end of April. What happens then I don't know, as with luck, the airships will then be once more Naval in which case I shall still be with them, quite likely at Howden, East Fortune near Edinburgh or Pulham in Norfolk which are the only places staying on.

If the airships go back to the Air Force I don't know what will happen, except that I shall become a Captain R.A.F. instead of Major, which I only hold while C.O. here. I did not spend much time here after my Xmas leave, departing four days later to Middleton in the Wolds for a week, York for three days and three dances, then Barlow near Selby for four days and then back here. After that I settled down here for a few weeks with the exception of two nights away, when I went to York and Rugby respectively for dances – rather energetic.

Since then I went for a round tour one weekend, Rugby one night and dance, seeing R.E. and Margery, Brackley for one night, London Bedford for two nights then out to Watford to see R.E. at the Bourne's for the afternoon and back here on the night train. Since then I have been pretty busy starting the closing down of the station and demobilising half the men and officers, but found time for a good bit of hockey and have started golf again, but with not much success and a good bit of ball losing.

I am hoping to have my Austin Coupe in May, but have had no definite date yet and it may be a bit later. Still I saw the other day that the first of the new cars were finished so with luck I shall have it before the holidays are over. Last week I had a very good run in my R.A.F. 25/30 Crossley. Starting from here on the Saturday afternoon I went down to Aberystwyth (120 miles) for dinner and the night, on the next morning down to Pembroke (80 miles) the next afternoon back to Aberystwyth for dinner and the night and back again the following morning (about 400 miles). I left my driver behind and took an officer with me and, with the exception of one puncture, had a very good run.

Much love to you all from your affectionate brother Thomas. W. Elmhirst.

From Vic.   Winthorpe,
                                    38 Craven Road,
                                    Reading.
                                    July 29th [1919]

Dear Family,

I take up my pen with sad regret to see this Budget back in this untimely time. I think as the space has to be filled I will just have to put in a record of my doings since about the last time, when I arrived at Sunderland.

After I had been there about a month I was told I was a fool not to apply for embarkation leave before it was too late so one Tuesday I thought I would. I got off the mornings work, went off to the Adjutant and made my request. He said, "Of course you haven't had yours, you can have 6 days. Go upstairs and get meat & sugar cards and you can go off tonight if you like". I rushed off to the station and found a train getting to Crewe at 2 AM the next morning and so telegraphed to Mother, who I had just heard was at Rhosnigr[1], that I should arrive sometime that day (putting the wrong date unfortunately). I had a good journey though after Crewe, I did not sleep much.

In a conversation with the Guard at Crewe he told me that the train was too long stop in the station at Twy Croes (which was as near Rhosnigr as I could get, the station of the latter being shut) but if I came into the Van I could get out all right. So at Bangor, which is a junction just this side of the Menai Straits, I went into the Van and he pointed out all places of interest along the line. I was looking amongst the mail a little later and found an official letter to Tommy, thought of putting 'Censored j.v.e' but thought that he probably wouldn't have seen it, so didn't.

At Twy Croes there was no conveyance (5.30 AM) so by my friend the Guard's advice I went on for breakfast and clean up at Holyhead, passing on the way a large building with "The BAY HOTEL" inscribed upon it! After a poor breakfast but a good clean up (I had a razor Alfie, also cleaning things) interval here as another fellow and I went 1¾ miles

---

1   Rosnigr is a village on Anglesey.

to the Baths to find that they were shut!! I got a train back without paying of course and arrived at the Hotel at 8.30. Out popped Leonard's head from a window, for once he was down before breakfast!!!! I got in another breakfast then and afterwards went a walk up the river. After lunch we were all going by carriage to Tommy's Command and we did get off by about 3 pm though I made them rather late as I went to sleep on a sand bank about 30 yds in front of the Hotel, and they spent a long time searching the surrounding country for me! We had an excellent tea when we got there though our feet did stick to the carpet with the tar we brought in from the Rd.

We saw some of Irene's groups with criticisms then went round the sheds just in time to see one fellow make a bad landing so we are told. Coming from the sheds Tommy was pinked by a military knut but escaped to say goodbye. Later on Tommy got over the dinner and with Grandpa[2], we built an efficient bridge across the river, which lasted until we left; and anyhow longer than any previous bridge of its kind. It was about 13 yards long and was continually used by the inmates of the Hotel afterwards though at high tide it was covered. Leonard and I saw an elderly gent & wife trying to cross by it when the water was about 2 ft above it. It caused them some discomfort and us some unseen laughter. We made a few lady friends, Leonard two and me one as you may perhaps have heard and altogether we had a nice slack time there.

On the way back, at Holyhead we met Cousin Richard[3] with a camouflaged yacht as a sub chaser also Mr Guy (including another of Leonard's ladies) and at the last moment Tommy with a face like nothing on earth on account of a tooth. Later in the day we had to change stations at Manchester and, while Daddy & Mother went on, Leonard and I did hot work as porters. Unfortunately I did not know that a certain lunch basket, which was in the van, was ours so I left it behind, finding afterwards that it contained a leg of mutton and a

---

2 'Grandpa' is Leonard's family name.
3 Richard Elmhirst, the superintendent of Millport Marine Biology Station in the Firth of Clyde, was a first cousin of WHE and godfather to AOE. During the war he was commissioned into the R.N.V.R and served mainly in the Dover Patrol as a Lieutenant.

cheese!!! A Porter came along then and took our barrer off and we also went off at the double across a few lines until at last we got to the train. We walked down the train but Mother & Daddy weren't there as we had raced them, and as we turned back the train went off; just at the end we saw them leaning out of the window and Daddy threw us our tickets.

We then took the luggage about a mile by taxi to a 3rd station and in about ¾ hour took our seats (1st class) getting home about 6 pm. If our train had not been late we should have got home before them; we spent the evening watering the garden and the next day I had to depart at 10 pm sleeping from 12 to 4 AM at York, getting to Sunderland in time for work. That morning, Wednesday, a notice came round saying that any officer wishing to go in for a course of instruction in aviation was to send in his name to the Orderly Room. I thought this a good stunt so complied and on the Saturday was told to report at Newcastle at 10 AM on the following Monday. This I did and was told to report up in Hampstead somewhere on the following morning for medical inspection. I decided to call in at home on the way and I got in about 3 pm staying till 1.30 AM when I walked off to Cudworth to catch the 3.30 train to town. I got a good dish o'tea at Cudworth with a telegraph clerk in front of a fire and later got off; arriving in town about 9.30 am and going straight to Hampstead where I took my place in a queue for handing our papers in, which I did by about 10.30. Then I went upstairs and by 1 o'clock had been to about 3 rooms in which I had spent about 2 minutes each time. From 2 pm to 4 pm I went through one more room and got a certificate given me as fit for a Pilot.

I had heard from Mother that Leonard was in the Inns of Court A.T.S. at Gidea Park, but found there were no Inns of Court there but only Artists Rifles, still I thought I might try and so went to Paddington to find my way to it. I had to go right across London again to the right station and was then so tired I thought of giving it up, you see I really did not think Leonard would be there and if he was I was doubtful of finding him, also I had only had two eggs since dinner the day before. Still I went on, and got there at last and after getting into conversation with 1 Sergt Kospe (?) and 1 Pte. The latter took me in turn to the Orderly Rooms and to my enormous surprise he had heard of Leonard's hut, shouted for Elmhirst and said an <u>officer</u> wanted to speak to him. Out rushed Leonard to be completely diddled by the sight of me! We then sat and talked a bit under a tree & then he took me off to the cricket ground where he was just going to play. After a mouthful of Irene's favourite (Gum not Arabic) I watched him go in to make one valiant 4 and then come out to such a nice one.

(Tuesday. Just back from Signalling 6.30 – 7.30!!!) After that I went to the station jumped into a train and just before it went off, jumped out to go and see where it was going to. At Romford I saw some buses on the road so got out of the train and started off by bus, thinking I should be back in town with ½ hour run about, 9.30 pm. I found it took 1¾ hours so was rather late, but went off to the G.C. Hotel as soon as I could. I walked into the place, got into a queue of officers who I thought must all be wanting rooms or something until I found the Hotel had been turned into a Hospital, so I backed out and went off to the Station Hotel at Paddington that I found was full up and I went to Berners Hotel finding a room there at about 12 midnight. I soon got to bed though I had a bath first although of course I had no sleeping or washing kit of any kind.

The next morning I got breakfast and my belt etc cleaned, went off & got a haircut bought a few things and went off at about 1 pm to Brackley where I spent till 7 pm with Irene eating most of the time. At tea I decided to take another day off and visit Richie.

Irene suggested phoning for a bed and after doing so I saw her off and arrived at Rugby about 10 pm. Richie was just off to bed so I went also (slept in Cousin C's pyjamas); without seeing him. Next morning he was working so I only saw him for about ¾ hour then I went off home. A porter at Sheffield told me to stay in till Penistone which I did getting there about 2 pm and finding there was a train to Barnsley at about 5 pm!! So I set out to walk. It was a hot day and I was sorry that I had even brought a British Warm. Still, at Dodworth I got a seat in a bread van and got home about 4.30 in time for tea. As far as I can remember I spent the evening watering strawberries and at 10 pm I went off to Sunderland.

On Friday & Saturday the men were doing nothing having been inoculated so I had nothing much to do, but I was warned for a Gas Course on Monday at a place 4 miles away. Had to walk there every morning coming back about 4.30. This lasted 4 days, but we had an interval on Wednesday as there was a 'Stand To'. As a matter of fact we had heard that it would take place on Tuesday night so we all stayed up, some the whole night & some (with me) till about 1.30 when we went to bed. Of course the alarm came then at about 2.30 and we had to get up and dress and rush off after the rest of the Coy who had had the alarm ½ hour earlier. We marched about 5 miles till we came to the cliffs where we had our posts and I spread my platoon along about a mile of cliff as out of sentries. There we stayed till about 3 pm the men getting two meals at 9 am & 2 pm and officers one at 9. I was slightly lucky as a party of people whom I had met at Canon Sykes' tennis party came for a picnic to the bit of cliff in my charge. I made a nice meal with eggs sandwiches and cider!!!! and some of the men got some too. It was a tiring day as I must have wandered up and down my bit of front about 10 times and it was nearly a mile long.

The next two were GAS again & on the Sunday I received a notice telling me to report at Reading as soon as possible. I got off the next morning at 7am, lost my luggage at York, but got home for tea and the night (watering raspberries in the evening).

Started by trap for Cudworth about 6 am next morning and reported at Reading at about 4 pm. They had no room for me there so sent me off on 12 days leave. I went back to the station got my luggage (it had arrived before me) and went off to town, dropped my stuff at St Pancras got a room at 'Dean Hotel' Oxford Street an excellent place only 6/- for bed & breakfast, and then got a theatre. The next day I had a shave went to Cox's etc and got theatre tickets which I went to in the afternoon & evening also a Cinema.

About midnight I got my train and arrived at Cudworth about 5.30 am. I had telegraphed home so that they might meet me about 6.15 but I found there was a mail train at 6 am so got in it leaving a message for the trap if it was coming. Just as we left the station I saw the trap in the distance but it came back all right to Barnsley and landed me and the luggage in time for breakfast. I then spent 10 days working like any nigger, though much blacker, and at times with more scent as I bespattered myself well with soup!! (I heard from Miss C that she & Irene plugged their nasal organs with lavender when they worked at it!!!) On Saturday July 6th I reported again at Reading and actually got a billet, and a good one, but on Monday morning we were all told to go on 6 days leave again as the instructors had flue [sic].

This time I left my luggage and spent the afternoon & night at Marlborough going on the next morning and getting home about 2 pm. I had sent an expressed letter home announcing my coming and Daddy got it, but Mother spied it amongst some of his letters in her usual manner. The great thing was that Leonard had come home on sick leave that morning and we neither of us knew about each other. Anyhow I found they had gone to Leek's wood for raspberries so followed picking up Conus at Jarrett Spring!! I came on them in the wood. They had got about 6 Raspberries but both clippers, so I continued the good work. We went on to Aunty Min for tea, eating her out very nearly. What disgusted me most was the way Leonard ate, it was really shocking!!!! Leonard & I spent the next 4 days hard at work irrigating and eating Loganberries etc. On Friday he went off to Psalmist & on Saturday I followed. I nearly came back without boots bag etc as I had not packed till the morning and slept rather late; my breakfast being at about 7 something too. Still I did my boots up in the trap & polished belt & buttons on the way to Penistone & Sheffield. At Nottingham I picked up a Civilian & Staff Officer and, leaving the latter to his lunch, we descended at Brackley where we spent several restive & instructive hours which I cannot write upon etc etc ------ !!!

After missing that lovely [quite true] train at Rugby I got off about 12 on Sunday, saw the Naval Pictures in town and got to Reading about 8 pm and on Monday really started work.

On the Friday however I got a chit telling me to report at the Office at 6pm for Inoculation. There was a queue of about 50 waiting there with sleeves rolled up and a patch of iodine on the shoulder. I took my place, and had a large tube dug about half an inch into my arm and then went away, having been told that I was excused for the Sat & Sun. I racked my brains and decided to go to Winchester the next day. I did a mornings work on Sat. as we should only have had to make it up another time and then went off to the station with 1 pair of pyjamas in my pocket. I had telegraphed to Pom to meet me but missing my train at Basingstoke had 1¾ hrs to wait so telegraphed to him again. I arrived there about 4.30 pm he took me to 'YE ANCIENT HOTEL' where we got a rotten tea. Then we went up to Why not ring!!!! (Good) and found Hales & Jimmy (most garments) and took them off to dinner which was a good one and afterwards strolled back to house again, Pom giving me his razor as I appeared to be rather hairy. I also had nothing to clean my bootons, didn't half get ticked off, nearly as bad as Leonard. That's the worst of having relations who think themselves soldiers (Vanity of Vanities is what I calls them). Next morning I had a shave & breakfast, polished my shoes with the curtains and went off to find Alfie, who was also on his way to find me. I collected Jimmy & Hales and found Alfie on my way back, wandered round their patch of grasses (called a cricket field) till the bell <u>rang</u> (Oh Alfie, I haven't a notion). Then went to Chapel. Afterwards I saw Mr Broomfield then went off with Pom, Pearson & Bernard (2 more of his little chums) to lunch & smoke, afterwards getting J & H and going for a walk. I broke my beloved stick & bought another (which got entangled in some railings two days later & broke)! We all had tea then & rushed off for evening chapel. I went to see Matron later then left Pom to go Rugby? and took a walk (borrowing 10/- from Alfie to pay my bill). Which I paid back though he declines to write & thank me so never call me safe again.

Got up at 6 on Monday caught train getting back here just in time for work at 9 am. I'm having quite a good time here and as usual am working really hard. Working hours are from 6.30 – 7.30 9 – 12.30 2 – 5.45 and we are <u>supposed</u> to copy out & learn our notes in our spare time. Yesterday there was a match between us & some other team. We were practically told 'you must either buy a ticket & watch or parade as usual', and as I did not trouble to get a ticket I paraded!!!

The first 2 weeks my work consisted of Rigging Aeroplanes & truing them up taking off wings etc Bomb dropping with safety devices & fuses. Instruments such as Compasses, Cameras, Pressure Gauges & Wireless Instruments, Theory of Flight Lewis Guns & Signalling. The next 2 weeks are Engines, Vickers guns & signalling. The former is good. I try to learn about Carburetion, Magnetos etc, the last being very hard on my poor cranium. You should have seen me yesterday with a 250 HP Rolls Royce 12 cylinder getting it up to 1500 revolutions per min. The thing was stationary of course but excellent sport.

The last fortnight consists of Aerial Navigation which I think deals with Allowances for wind, Compass bearings etc, after that I shall go to some training squadron and learn to fly also I hope to get flying pay!! Well if this is not enough for anyone please tell me though I doubt if anyone will read the whole. With luck I hope to get home after the course if I am not put back to another one for failing in some of the exams which is quite on the cards. I might learn a bit more then too. I went for a row on the river yesterday about 4 miles down stream and back in my little Rob Roy[4].

<u>Irene.</u> Remember that photo of you also what was that name you called Miss -----?

<u>Alfie.</u> I await your thanks & receipt or you will need reseating.

<u>Richie.</u> Nothing

<u>Tommy.</u> Got the brass hat & socks yet I shouldn't mind a leg & arm photo, if one to spare.

<u>Vic.</u> You darling what a lovely letter you have written to be sure.

<u>Leonard</u> Where's your letter I can't find it except <u>the prehistoric</u> one.

<u>Monday</u> Bank holiday or something. Anyhow we did have the afternoon off to watch some sports. The day after my real ripping Rob Roy row I went to the river again and found the only thing left was a skiff, +

---

4   A small kayak.

sliding seat etc, about twice as easy to upset as a canoe. I got in thinking I should get along nicely but after pushing out I found I was about as safe as----well Irene eating strawberries at Brackley! I thought I was in for a bathe but <u>gradually</u> (very) I improved and at last got up the river as far as Pangbourne about 6½ miles, had tea there and came back in better style in 1¼ hrs. Going up through a lock we had a funny time keeping everyone waiting as we (another fellow who joined me with like boat) had no control over our boats and upset unless we had the oars straight out or held on to some thing. The thing was about 20 ft long by 2 broad and 1 deep. The Crabs I caught came to about 5 in 7 strokes as per: we have had 5 days without rain since we came.

Well Cherio Chin Chin I Wipe tears from My Eye

Your doting

Vic   Jve

Drawing of men on beds from Vic's letter of 29th July 1919.

10 am the 5th June and all standing by for Dr's rounds. The man at the end is not a corps though you might think it. His neighbour's nose-bridge has an extra bump in it by mistake. Diseases represented; sand fly and malaria and no one very bad. I'd have put a sister in but they never stay quite long enough to enable the lightening artist to get anything but a good impression (in his mind). The corps at the end is unnaturally shrivelled, the 2nd down is an excellent illustration of that telling expression "work to a thread".

Note – The above paragraph and the drawing on page 204 was firmly clipped to Vic's original letter of 29th July 1919, but the context suggests it may belong with a missing letter from Mesopotamia written in June 1920.)

From Leonard.   S.S. Vauban.
                                 October 12th 1919

Dear Tommy, V.R.A. and I.

Here beginneth the second chapter of the <u>Family Budget</u>, and I hope you will not mind the typewriting, for there is a very good reason for it. I sent my young fortune over to America in front of me in order that I should not starve for a few days at least when I arrived over there, then I had to borrow enough to see me across. This morning I made a fair start by enquiring of the purser on board whether he had any work for me, at least I did not do it, a friend did the asking and I merely walked in a few minutes later and the purser who is not a bad fellow, having enquired whether I was likely to be ill all the way across said he was hard up for a typist and would keep me busy and square it with a fiver at the end of the voyage which will last another six days at least, our old boat being a trifle slow. It makes up for this by being very palatial.

I have a state room to myself, with a window, none of your wretched port holes, and I can be ill in here whenever I like without arousing undue curiosity. Added to this we have a first rate orchestra to play to us at lunch and dinner times, a gymnasium has given me riding cycling and rowing all within five minutes, as well as massage from a fearsome electrical machine which slams you violently in the belly at a great rate. As for the passengers they are rather a dud lot and not a single pretty girl amongst them, it so happens that my chair is situated within a yard of the only one that is at all presentable but that of course was not my fault. Both Smoke room and drawing room have beautiful open fires, lots of coal, and plenty of the necessary receptacles for the benefit of the expectorating Americans.

As for the food, we might be having our meals at the Carlton or Monsieur Jammets in Dublin except that there are a number of odd dishes which one does not meet in our parts, I generally miss them at first and either have to bring them in at the end or else go back one or two and have them over again including the omitted delicacy. What about buckwheat cakes and maple syrup, or puffed rice and grape fruit. They're bully, Gee, but it's a swell ship. Do you think I shall pass as a professional typist for the Cunard company. By the way, up to date it has been as calm as a mill pond, the last land we sighted was called the Dodran, etc, and I've just been giving riding lessons on the motor gee gee.

I had breakfast with Richie in his rooms at Cambridge, the first he had ever given, dined with him in his hall and generally had a good time. The next you will hear about him is that he has been having the princes round to coffee, since I gather he is to be elected to the same select club which they will attend. I say you chaps it's a beastly swiz, I wish I was going up again like a festive new bug (new expression, from Charterhouse I think) Golly, but I'll give him a juicy biff when I get home for the hols.

I gather Pom has arranged about his motor cycle all right and what about Miss Mitchell. Is that her name? I've also heard about some wonderful shooting by him[1] and Richie. Nothing's safe from us now, if only we could spend another Irene's birthday on the Moor, how many braces would we not have to our bags? I think that I have got my eye in rather well for tomorrow, don't you? So, no more now, I can already feel that five pounds rattling in my pocket, except that since Pom's worn my suit there's a terrible rend in the bottom of it. The music has started, I'm off.

Leonard

---

1 Pom wrote a letter to his mother dated 20th July 1919 in which he described the victory of his house cricket team in the Winchester house competition (Pom was captain), as well as his part (as 9th man and marker) in the Winchester shooting XIII which carried off the Ashburton Shield at Bisley. The cup was presented by Prince Albert (Bertie). On arriving back at Winchester the shooting XIII were expecting a quiet walk back to school, but on pulling into the station they were amazed to hear a roar of voices. the whole school was waiting outside. Pom and the whole XIII were lifted onto shoulders and carried back to school in triumph. A week later the cup was presented by Bertie with more ceremony.

From Vic.　　　　　　　　　The Tigris at about Aziziyah
　　　　　　　　　　　　　　Halfway between Kut and Baghdad
　　　　　　　　　　　　　　13th Nov 1919

Dear Brethren,

(In this land the females quite rightly do not count). I hope this leaves you as it finds me in the height of pinkness, so much so that I do this almost incredible task of writing for F.B. May the days of its coming shorten, before the said and heretofore mentioned epistle has yet perchanced to intrude upon my ken.

W.O., Arretez, likewise (below the steamer hoots, for what reason? I must find out) One cannot afford to lose any excitement that's going these days. Only passing another boat, but I just stayed out to see us tie up to the bank for the night. We have to do this because, even in daylight, we run on one or two a day. I feel like giving a lengthy description of this voyage, over which we have spent two months, but I don't know whether it will interest you. Still, the chief thing is to get this letter written.

We actually left England on the date we had been told i.e. Sept 19th to do which, we paraded at about the usual hour for these moves, that is, about 2.15 am. After some thought, I have decided on diary form. (Ant going up my sleeve. A crowd of about 80 like him have just removed a cricket I squashed on the wall last night.)

19th. Paraded 2.15 and marched to the station, men singing mournful tunes with great gusto. The train starts, but after 100 yards, stops as someone had pulled the chain. After 10 minutes it is decided that it was an accident (no lights being on) and we again start, the bugles playing the advance. All goes well for half an hour and most people have got to sleep, including me who, with another fellow being Colour Bearers, get a carriage to ourselves, when the same thing happens again. This time the engine driver tried to ignore it and broke a coupling, leaving half the train behind, but after that all went well till 8 am when an axle overheated and the carriage had to be removed. I woke up. This was Peterborough or somewhere in Cambridge though we were supposed to be in Tilbury then.

The buglers would play reveillez till we got into London on a little by-line when we could see everyone having breakfast. They then turned up with the rations and gave the cook house call. On getting to Tilbury we found we had to go by ferry to the boat which was in mid-stream. I had to go with the Colours and some idiot sent my tin suit case (the only absolutely necessary baggage for the whole voyage) down to the hold where about a ton of soda water bottles in crates were placed on top of it. I lived for over a week by borrowing razor, hairbrush etc and not changing until, in sorting out the hold, I chanced to spot and rescue it.

I got a nice little cabin, with two other fellows, containing 3 bunks, 2 wash hand stands, 2 chests of drawers and 1 wardrobe. It sounds big, but was only about 7 foot by 12 so that when you got some luggage in you could hardly put a foot on the ground. Still it was quite comfortable and had a good fan, the only other trouble being that it was near the engine room.

At 4 pm we started down the river, all seeming quite cheerful and everything went well. On the next day however-

20th We got into the channel with a bit of a swell and I spent the day doing immense speed up and down the deck to prevent any ill feeling. I must have done at least 10 miles and it succeeded in so far that I could eat and passably enjoy my meals.

21st We got into the bay and now began to corkscrew in an objectionable fashion, which quickly brought my downfall, though I managed to eat breakfast and dinner. I then went down and stayed there after till next morning.

22nd Now we began to get off the Spanish coast the sea became nicer and we felt an enjoyable warmth. We saw our first porpoises and also heaps of people who had not appeared above deck before!

23rd Passed quite close to the Portuguese coast with everyone airing their knowledge of geography and finding it all wrong. If I'd only had my camera out I'd have got some photos of the coast and mountains which looked like those we once saw on the other side of Schehallion and also of Gibraltar where we arrived in the afternoon. Here we had our first encounter with the little boys selling grapes, apples etc, all at extortionate prices, which the men were quite pleased to give as they would be a distinct change after the ordinary ration. We left that evening and, keeping in the sight of land, got to Marseilles on the 26th.

Stayed there 3 days with nothing to do as we were not allowed off the ship and were all pleased to be off again towards Malta. Since then we have seen no rain and not many clouds. And with it being a bit damp we've all felt the heat horribly, perspiring all the time. At Malta we stopped the afternoon and Lord Plumer, who was in the Regiment, came on board and inspected his guard of honour and chatted a bit. The crowd of cameras, which faced him when he appeared up the gangway, was enough to send him off again. All that he could see was about 12 people bending over their cameras clicking away hard. That evening we left again (we've just run on a sand bank, but only slightly) and on the 3rd arrived at Port Said. Here the little boys would dive for anything, the aristocrats at Malta would only look at silver!

I was on watch in the evening when we started through the canal with our search light on. The desert looked everything and more than I had expected, though the line of barbed wire along the north bank looked quite out of place. We had thought to find the heat terrible here, but it wasn't half bad especially as we had just begun wearing our drill suits. However, when we got well into the Red Sea we went down with a following wind and simply got it in the neck. Everyone tried to sleep, but as it was about 103 in the cabins and, on the actual side of the ship, 120, you just lay down and perspired. Not that it made you damp, because it immediately evaporated. Still, we only got one day of that and afterwards it was quite pleasant again.

When not working there were deck games and we had a gymkhana, Regimental sports and boxing, so that what with the truly magnificent quality and quantity of the food, I could have continued to live there with pleasure for six months or more. The less said about the feeding the better I think. For example, a dish would come on one side of the table (6 subalterns), but it would never pass more than 4. I think I sent Irene some of the menus.

On the 8th we arrived at Aden,[1] (I hope to remember to put a photo in; in my last letter home I perjured myself by saying there were some enclosed). Just after we had left we heard we shouldn't be going to Bombay, but to Karachi. I wondered how my letters would go on, but they seem to have arrived all right, at least four have done, two of which came from Brackley for which I have sent multitudinous thanks, they being easier to send than a separate letter!

About the 13th Oct we arrived in Karachi and with much sorrow we left our cricket-infested cabin. The little beasts were awfully sharp and would steal your biscuits in the morning if you laid them down a moment. They also chirp all night and have a liking for walking on the pillow. Otherwise we were free from any insects whatsoever. At Karachi we stayed for two weeks in a rest camp North West of the town. It was very hot and dusty, but it's a dry heat which did not inconvenience one when out of the sun. We were all in tents provided with stone floor, beds and mosquito curtains. As a matter of fact there was a colony of small ants under the floor who were extremely interesting, but rather in the way. They could find their way anywhere and into anything. A pack of biscuits sealed up in paper standing amidst a crowd of books etc on the table was found after ¾ of an hour to have a little double track of ants going from a hole in the floor, up the table leg, over about four books and into the biscuits – then all the way back again. We placed it then on a rack attached to the tent pole about 7 foot from the ground only to find the ants up and down the pole. Even inside a hut, hung on a peg from the rack, would not keep it untouched.

A large size in wasps put the wind up me one night as I will recount. In appearance it was like this.

Rather a good likeness, but not quite terrifying enough. I imagined it was a hornet, so was careful and taking my towel, rolled it up and hit the thing as hard as I could where it had settled on the side of the tent. It just dropped to a spot about 6 ins above my bed and began cleaning itself. I had at it again and it vanished, but that was worse still as I wanted to get

---

1 Vic actually wrote "Malta" in his letter, but must have meant Aden, which is half way between Port Said and Karachi.

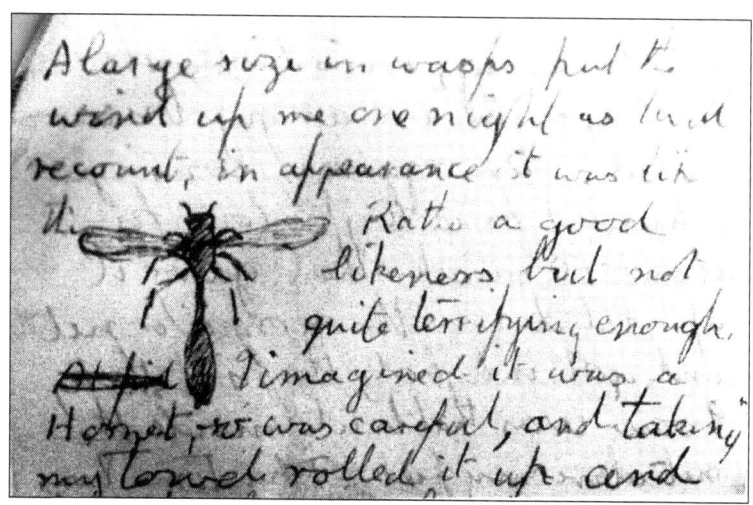

Vic's wasp referred to in his letter 13th November.

to bed, so I took the lamp and hunted through the bed clothes, under the bed then I suddenly saw it on a wooden frame. I seized a book and smacked it down on it and slid it along. Immediately it flew up with an angry buzz – I fled. On regaining courage I hunted for it high and low for about 10 minutes then gave it up, let down the mosquito net and got into bed. The first thing I saw was that brute inside the net above my feet. This time I was lucky. I caught him in a fold of the net and with a knife, cut off his head and a wing and slipped him in a matchbox to give evidence of my tale. Of course, next morning the matchbox was filled with two wings, some legs and ants!

Landed at Permanent Camp 12 miles from Baghdad. Christmas mail just going. This is 1st edition F.B., but haven't managed to write another letter for home.

Vic.

EPILOGUE

For people like me, who knew all these writers as my uncles and aunt when I was growing up (except for Willie and Christie of course), it is fascinating to try and match the boy (or girl) with the man (or woman) they became.

Their letters, written almost a century ago, still seem fresh and spirited even though the world they described has changed beyond all recognition. In fact, it was changing as they wrote. Cars, aeroplanes and telephones were a novelty. The horse, the train and the bicycle were how you travelled in the country if you did not walk and they did plenty of walking.

Most of all, the social order was about to change, but it was still clear who the privileged were. Thanks mainly to the coal that lay under the estate consisting of some 500 acres (part of which had been in the possession of the family since the early 14th Century), the Elmhirst children were educated by a string of governesses until they were old enough to go to prep school. Later they all went to various public schools where, according to Willie and Richard, they were all miserable and longed for the holidays. Their father saw university as an unnecessary luxury for those younger sons destined for the army or the professions.

At home someone else did the cooking, the cleaning, the waiting, the gardening, the labouring and the grooming (the groom underwent a few hours of re-training to be turned into the chauffeur when Papa Elmhirst bought his first car in 1914) and, of course, someone else dug the coal out.

Only Leonard, in his letter of 7th June 1914, refers to the plight of those at the bottom of the social woodpile. The Russian Revolution was yet to come.

I have attached a map to enable readers to make sense of the geography of Worsbrough and to find the various houses owned by the family, two of which can be glimpsed from the M1 motorway that now cuts through the heart of the estate. The photographs speak for themselves. I have added a shortened version of the family tree to help family readers and others to identify most of the cousins, aunts and uncles referred to in the letters. I also hope that these lively letters will open a window on to those times and events which are already sinking into the sediment of ancient history. With today's tidal wave of internet communication and small families we are unlikely to see another collection quite like the Family Budget.

Finally, for those of you who never knew the grown-up versions of the writers, I have added short biographies (or, perhaps, "Brief Lives" in the manner of John Aubrey) and some later photographs of the brothers and their sister, together with a few old family stories which may otherwise be forgotten. The greatest surprise to Papa and Mama must have been Leonard's marriage to Dorothy Whitney Straight and their subsequent creation (with the help of Dorothy's money and inspiration) of a remarkable community at Dartington Hall in Devon. But although Dartington did not deflect Tommy, who reached the top in his chosen profession, it is certain that the lives of Vic, Richard and Pom would have been very different had there been no Dartington and no financial assistance from Leonard and Dorothy. We can only speculate as to what William and Christie might have achieved had they survived the war.

WILLIAM ELMHIRST

Willie as a young boy.

Born 9th Jan 1892 at the Vicarage, Laxton, in the East Riding of Yorkshire, Willie was educated at home by various governesses until he was sent to Stancliffe Hall prep school at Matlock. He was then sent to Malvern College. In 1911 he went up to Worcester College, Oxford. After graduating he was articled to his Uncle Charles, a solicitor practising in York. With the onset of war, he volunteered for the army and, in October 1914, was commissioned as a second Lieutenant and posted to the East Yorkshire Regiment. The Regiment was sent to France and took part in the Battle of the Somme. He wrote his last F.B. letter (as a captain) on the 26th Oct 1916 to say that he was going up to the trenches in 'a rather unhealthy spot'. He wrote in his last letter to his mother on the 6th Nov 1916: "Out here one becomes so used to the idea of death, and that in most unpleasant forms, that it comes to seem a very small thing indeed. I have seen some far from pleasant sights during the last few days, but it is astonishing how little it affects one, though it takes people in very different ways." A week later, on the 13th November 1916, he was killed in action at Serre. He was 24 years old. His remains are buried in the cemetery at Serre.

Willie as a young man.

We know that he wrote two diaries. The first he wrote at Malvern, but on his death it was read by his father who was horrified by what he found. "If I had ever realised the kind of suffering he was being put through at

Malvern, I'd have taken him away immediately and no one shall ever read this again," he said. He then threw the diary on the fire. The other diary, which did survive, was kept during his first year as a freshman at Worcester College, Oxford. That diary, which describes the life of an average Oxford student in 1911-12, was published in 1969 by Basil Blackwood, Oxford. It is called 'A Freshman's Diary 1911-12'

Like the rest of his brothers, Willie was introduced to cricket and shooting at an early age. They also tended their pets. Thus, when his baby brother Edward died, Willie and Leonard (then aged 6 and 5) prepared his grave in the corner of the garden where they usually buried their deceased pets only to watch with horror as his coffin was taken across the road, to be buried in the churchyard.

If school was misery, the holidays were paradise in comparison. As the eldest, Willie was in command of his brothers as they re-enacted battles of the Boer War (the youngest boys, of course, having to be satisfied with the role of defeated Boers). Willie seems to have been an enthusiastic student at Oxford where he attended church, played a variety of sports, read novels and visited the Ashmolean Museum. He formed close relationships with his fellow (male) students and tutors, learned Italian and took guitar lessons. It is hard to tell from the diary whether he gave much thought to the political developments of the time, but my guess is that he did not. Like hundreds of other public schoolboys of that time, he had been a member of the school O.T.C. and when war was declared he volunteered to do his duty. He died, as a captain, leading his men to their doom.

In Memory of

W Elmhirst

Captain
8th Bn., East Yorkshire Regiment
who died on
Monday, 13th November 1916. Age 24.

Additional Information: Son of the Rev. W. H. Elmhirst, of "Elmhirst", Barnsley, Yorks. Educated at Malvern College and Worcester College, Oxford.

Commemorative Information

Cemetery: SERRE ROAD CEMETERY No. 1, Pas de Calais, France

Grave Reference/Panel Number: I. D. 4.

Location: The village of Serre is 11 kilometres north-north-east of Albert. Using the D919 from Arras to Amiens you will drive through the villages of Bucquoy, Puisieux then Serre-Les Puisieux (approximately 20 kilometres south of Arras). On leaving Serre Les Puisieux, 700 metres further along the D919, Serre Road No.1 Cemetery can be found on the right hand side.

Historical Information: The "Serre Road" was, in June 1916, the road out of Mailly-Maillet to Serre and Puisieux, which entered No Man's Land about 1,280 metres South-West of Serre. The 31st and 4th Divisions attacked North and South of this road on the 1st July, 1916. Parties of the 31st Division reached Serre; but the attack failed, and the 3rd and 31st Divisions attacked again, without success, on the 11th November. On the 24th February, 1917, the Germans evacuated Serre, and on the following morning the 22nd Manchesters entered it. In the spring of 1917, the battlefields of the Ancre were cleared by the V Corps and a number of cemeteries made, three of which are now named from the Serre Road. On the 25th March, 1918, Serre was evacuated by the British, and the cemeteries fell into enemy hands; but on the following 14th August, it was in turn evacuated by the Germans. The cemetery was made by the V Corps in May, 1917, when Plot I, Row A to G, were filled; but it was greatly enlarged after the Armistice by the concentration of graves (for the most part, of 1916) from the battlefields of the Ancre and the Somme. There are now nearly 2,500, 1914-18 war casualties commemorated in this site. Of these, nearly three quarters are unidentified and special memorials are erected to ten soldiers from the United Kingdom, known or believed to be buried among them. Other special memorials record the names of twelve soldiers from the United Kingdom, buried in other cemeteries, whose graves were destroyed by shell fire. Two of the United States Army have been removed to other Cemeteries. The cemetery covers an area of 6,539 square metres and is enclosed by a rubble wall. Ninety one metres West of the cemetery is the HEBUTERNE-SERRE FRENCH NATIONAL CEMETERY ("Cimetiere Militaire Particulier D'Hebuterne-Serre"), made in 1920-21, to receive the bodies of the dead of two French Infantry Regiments, the 243rd and the 327th (both raised at Lille), who fell in the Combat of Hebuterne on the 10th-13th June, 1915. It

Page 1 of the commemorative information about Willie.

rises in terraces to a stone screen wall, carrying a bronze memorial in relief. The Battle Memorials of the 1st Royal Scots Fusiliers (3rd Division) and the 12th York and Lancaster Regiment (31st Division) are in the immediate neighbourhood. The following were among the burial grounds from which British graves were concentrated to Serre Road Cemetery No. 1:- ACHEUX COMMUNAL CEMETERY FRENCH EXTENSION, in which two soldiers from the United Kingdom were buried in April and May, 1916. ALBERT GERMAN CEMETERY ("am Nordwest Ausgang") (now removed), where 18 soldiers from the United Kingdom were buried in April and May, 1918. BEAUCOURT-SUR-ANCRE BRITISH CEMETERY (V Corps Cemetery No. 13), in the middle of the village, containing the graves of 21 officers and men from the United Kingdom who fell in November, 1916. February, 1917. CERISY-BULEUX CHURCHYARD, in which one soldier from the United Kingdom was buried in November, 1916. PUISIEUX CHURCHYARD, where two soldiers from the United Kingdom were buried by the enemy in September, 1915. TEN TREE ALLEY CEMETERY No. 1, PUISIEUX (V Corps Cemetery No. 24), 640 metres South-East of Serre, which contained the graves of 37 soldiers from the United Kingdom who fell in November, 1916-February, 1917. (The present Ten Tree Alley Cemetery was No. 2.)

Display Record of Commemoration

Page 2 of the commemorative information about Willie.

LEONARD KNIGHT ELMHIRST

Leonard as a boy with spaniel.

Born 6th June 1893 at the Vicarage, Laxton, Leonard died in California on the 16th April 1974 aged 80. Like his elder brother, he was educated by governesses before being sent to St Anselm's prep school and then to Repton where he inscribed in his diary the words, "1907, 1st term, MISERY, REPTON". In 1912 he entered Trinity College, Cambridge to read history in the expectation of being ordained (much to his mother's delight). There he joined the Student Christian Movement and became involved in Trinity's Camberwell Mission as well as the Y.M.C.A.

Under the influence of Goldsworthy Lowes Dickinson, Leonard began to question some of the orthodox thinking (religious and otherwise) that he had been brought up with. When he graduated in 1915, he did not join the army. He was passed as unfit by the family doctor, but, in any event, he was destined for the priesthood. He volunteered to work with the Y.M.C.A. in India, part missionary, part aid worker. From there he moved first to Basra and then to Amara in support of the Mesopotamia Expeditionary Force.

By 1917 he had clearer ideas. He decided to return to India and to renounce his plans to become a priest. There he met Lionel Curtis who had been sent to India by Prime Minister Lloyd George to work out a scheme whereby India would become a self-governing dominion within the British Commonwealth. Through Lionel Curtis, Leonard met another key figure to his future, Sam Higginbotham. Sam, an anti-sahib figure, had set out as a missionary, but he then realised that improved agricultural practice was essential if poverty and deprivation were to be alleviated. Sam told Leonard that he needed to understand more about modern agricultural methods if he wanted to improve life in India and that Cornell University in America was the place to study it.

In March 1918 Leonard sailed from India to England. Conscription had been introduced, but Leonard enlisted and, after a spell in the Officers Cadet Battalion of the Artists' Rifles[1], he was posted to Dublin in the Army Education Service, but only as a sergeant. To his regret he was never commissioned as an officer. However, by the summer he had been demobbed and might have returned to Barnsley to manage the family estate had Papa been ready for that. Papa was not ready, so Leonard took advice from Lionel Curtis and Michael Sadler and sailed for America.

On the 12th Oct 1919 Leonard wrote in the F.B. from S.S. Vauban en route to America and Cornell, "Here beginneth the second chapter of the Family Budget". And what a chapter it was to be! In fact, the Family Budget came to an end at this time as the various members of the family began their careers.

In his second semester at Cornell, Leonard was elected president of the Cosmopolitan Club, which provided accommodation for foreign students, but it was struggling with debt and facing closure. In his search for financial help Leonard managed to obtain an interview with Mrs Dorothy Whitney Straight, a young and extremely rich widow with three young children. He was 27, she was 33. By the end of October she had agreed to help with the problems of the Cosmopolitan Club.

He next saw her in April 1921 by which time he had met Rabindranath Tagore (a winner of the Nobel Prize for Literature and a world famous figure). Tagore was looking for someone who was willing to help him to tackle the problems of rural decline in India and who could help to revitalise those depressed communities both economically and creatively.

---

1 In "The Elmhirsts of Dartington" reference is made to Leonard being in the Officers' Cadet Battalion of the Coldstream Guards although his letter of 16th July 1918 is from the OTC of the 2nd Artists' Rifles. It is most likely that Sgt Baker of the Coldstream Guards was seconded to the 2nd Artists' Rifles to sharpen up their drill.

Tagore made no mention of funding, but soon after that meeting, while in New York, Leonard called unannounced on Dorothy at her palatial house on Fifth Avenue. There he asked her to support Tagore's project in India to which she agreed.

Leonard's relationship with Dorothy now began to develop in several ways. By the time he returned to India to become the director of Tagore's Institute for Rural Re-construction at Sriniketan the relationship was no longer purely a matter of business (at least in Leonard's mind). In January 1922 he wrote to Dorothy asking for more funds for the project and asking for her hand in marriage. "Marriage," she replied, "is out of the question", but money was forthcoming for the project. Their correspondence continued as they discussed Tagore and the project. They also discussed the possibility of further projects in America and England. Finally, after much correspondence, Leonard made a proposal that was accepted. They married in April 1925.

Leonard and Vic on the cricket field at Dartington.

After their marriage they bought Dartington Hall Estate in Devon, which became the venue for their English experiment in rural reconstruction, Leonard taking the initiative on matters agricultural and Dorothy on matters artistic and creative. Their experiment was deeply influenced by Tagore's ideas as well as their own. Some of those ideas were well formed and some were vague, but from them emerged something quite remarkable. One of the better-known projects was the school that I attended from 1950 to 1959. In the early days its radical and progressive methods were enjoyed by Leonard's three stepchildren, Whitney, Michael and Beatrice, as well as his own children, Ruth and William. I do not propose to describe or analyse all the subsequent developments at Dartington. (The full story

Leonard and Pom at Dartington 1972.

can be read in Michael Young's book, "The Elmhirsts of Dartington. The Creation of a Utopian Community" and in Victor Bonham-Carter's book "Dartington Hall – the History of an Experiment".)

The rest of Leonard's biography can be surveyed briefly from his entry in Who's Who. He was the President of the International Conference of Agricultural Economists from 1930 to 1961. He was chairman of the Political and Economic Planning think tank during the 1940s and a Devon County Councillor from 1939 to 1953. After Dorothy died in 1968, Leonard married Dr Susanna Isaacs (an ex-pupil of Dartington Hall School) and went to live with her in California, where he died in April 1974. His daughter Ruth died in 1986.

ERNEST CHRISTOPHER ELMHIRST

Born 25th December 1894 at the Vicarage, Laxton, Christie was educated by governesses before being sent to prep school at Stancliffe Hall and then to Malvern College. In one of his letters home (Sept 1909) he tells his parents, "Electric light has been installed at Malvern but there are not enough globes so it isn't very light in the studies".

Christie as a young man.

On leaving school he was articled to Fennell & Green, Mining Surveyors in Wakefield, which was the firm used by his father to check the removal of coal from under the Elmhirst estate. He volunteered for the Army at the outbreak of war and was commissioned as a 2nd Lieutenant in the 8th Duke of Wellington's Regiment in December 1914.

After training in England, his Regiment joined the British Mediterranean Expeditionary Force, with Christie having been appointed as a machine gun officer. His letter of 13th Feb 1915 recounts the ominous tale he had heard from an officer called Ince who had been in the trenches and who said: "If anyone gets killed it is the machine gun officer as the machine gun emplacement is shelled as soon as it is spotted." His brother Pom's comment for Christie in his F.B. letter of 12th May 1915 was equally ominous: "I hope you will have better luck than is prophesied, and remember to bring me a German helmet." (Perhaps Pom was unaware that Christie would be fighting the Turks.)

His last letter, which is not actually an F.B. letter, was written to his Auntie Min from an island close to the Dardanelles, describing the life in the camp there while he was waiting to be sent into action. Sadly, the prophecy proved correct. He was 20 years old when he was killed in action at Suvla Bay on the 11th August 1915.

Christie as a young subaltern in 1915.

Pom had a recollection of his mother coming into the bedroom, while the family was on a shooting holiday at Lassintullich in 1915, to tell him, Vic and Richard that, "the War Office is very sorry to say they don't know where Christie is." Christie's fate may explain the appearance of an item in the Barnsley Chronicle at that time which referred to the Rev W.H. Elmhirst "Offering an extra machine gun to Colonel Hewitt for the acceptance of the First Barnsley Battalion of the York & Lancaster "Old Pals" Regiment." Contributions were requested to add to the £102 already subscribed. Perhaps this ecclesiastical arms dealing had something to do with Papa Elmhirst's early ambition to become a soldier, which was thwarted by his father, a parson and a careful Yorkshireman no doubt, who dismissed the notion with the words, "I am not prepared to support a son of mine in a life of idleness."

In Memory of

Ernest Christopher Elmhirst

Second Lieutenant
8th Bn., Duke of Wellington's (West Riding Regt.)
who died on
Saturday, 7th August 1915. Age 20.

Additional Information: Son of the Rev. W. H. and Mrs. Elmhirst, of "Elmhirst," Barnsley.

Commemorative Information

Memorial: HELLES MEMORIAL, Turkey

Grave Reference/Panel Number: Panel 117 to 119

Location: The Helles Memorial stands on the tip of the Gallipoli Peninsula. It takes the form of an obelisk over 30 metres high that can be seen by ships passing through the Dardanelles. The memorial bears over 20,000 names and is both the memorial to the Gallipoli campaign and to men who fell in that campaign and whose graves are unknown or who were lost or buried at sea in Gallipoli waters (other than Australian and New Zealanders who are named on other memorials). Also inscribed on the memorial are the names of all the ships that took part in the campaign and the titles of the army formations and units which served on the Peninsula.

Historical Information: The Helles Memorial bears over 20,000 names and is both the memorial to the Gallipoli campaign and to men who fell in that campaign and whose graves are unknown or who were lost or buried at sea in Gallipoli waters (other than Australian and New Zealanders who are named on other memorials). Inscribed on it are the names of all the ships that took part in the campaign and the titles of the army formations and units which served on the Peninsula.

Display Record of Commemoration

Commemorative information about Christie.

THOMAS WALKER ELMHIRST

Born 15th December 1895 at the Vicarage, Laxton, Tommy was educated by governesses before being sent to prep school and then to the Royal Naval College, Osborne, on the Isle of Wight at the age of 12 ½ in the company of two future kings. (Queen Victoria had offered Osborne to the Navy to provide early training for the new breed of officers who would be needed to man the new Dreadnought battleships which were being built.) It says something for the well-hidden sensitivities of Papa that he recognised and encouraged Tommy's ambition to become a sailor, which was firmly established by the time Tommy was seven.

After Osborne he entered the Royal Naval College at Dartmouth. In May 1913 he passed out as a midshipman and was posted to the Dreadnought cruiser, H.M.S. Indomitable. He saw action in the Dardanelles and at the battle of the Dogger Bank. In February 1915 he was selected for "special service" and ordered to report to the Admiralty where he and fifteen other midshipmen were told by Lord Fisher, the First Sea Lord, that they had been selected to be captains of the new airships of the Royal Naval Air Service. Lord Fisher said: "Some of you will get the V.C. and some of you will be killed. If you don't want to fly, report back to this office within 48 hours." None did.

Tommy in his naval uniform in 1918.

Tommy's first task was to qualify as a balloon pilot. For his first night flight his balloon took off from the lawns of the Hurlingham Club in London. Once qualified as a pilot, his job was to fly his airship in search of German U boats in the seas around Britain, which he did for the next 3½ years. By 1918, at the age of 22, Tommy was in command of the Anglesey Naval Airship Station. (Shortly after armistice night he flew his SS Z73 under the Menai Straits Bridge for a dare.)

Tommy as an R.A.F. Wing Commander in 1930. (Note the A.F.C. medal awarded in 1918).

In 1920 Tommy was posted to command the R.A.F. Flying Boat base at Malta. (He would be taught how to fly a flying boat on arrival. "A week should be long enough," he was told). By 1936 Tommy was a Wing Commander looking after two bomber squadrons in Abingdon. From there he was posted to Ankara, as Air Attaché at the British Embassy, where he was able to enjoy fox hunting (Turkish style)[1] and to attend some of Ataturk's legendary parties. One of his missions was to try and persuade Turkey to join the Allies in the build up to WW II.

As the Battle of Britain began, Tommy, by now an Air Commodore, was placed in command of the Operations room. On his first day, alarming reports came in to say that 600 enemy aircraft were attacking British fighter airfields in Kent. After spending several months at Air Force House in Cairo, Tommy was sent to join the Desert Air Force as Second in Command to Air-Vice Marshal 'Maori' Cunningham with whom he remained until the Germans had been defeated at the battle of Alamein. Tommy was subsequently involved in "Operation Overlord" and in planning the invasion of Normandy.

In early 1947, Tommy was offered the job of Chief of Inter-Service Administration in India (then Pakistan and India) three months before

---

1 Tommy was invited to join the President's mounted guard on the barren Anatolian plateau. As he rode out wondering what would happen next, a figure ran forward and opened a sack containing a fox (courtesy of Ankara zoo). The assembled horsemen then galloped after the hapless fox as it ran off in search of some nonexistent cover.

partition and the hand over of India (under Nehru) and Pakistan (under Jinnah). As Tommy was preparing to leave, following the handover, he was offered the job of Chief of the new Indian Air Force. Perhaps one of the most onerous tasks of that appointment came out of the blue when Mahatma Gandhi was assassinated. Tommy, as Chief of Staff, was responsible for organising the funeral. He was given the news that morning on his return from a game of golf with his wife Katharine. The funeral, according to Hindu custom, would have to take place the following day and one million people were expected to attend. In his own words: "There was no time to be lost." He called up his fellow Chiefs of the Army and Navy, ordered whisky and soda, paper and pencils and set to work. The irony of a military man arranging the funeral of a world famous pacifist was not lost on Tommy.

Tommy as Governor of Guernsey escorting H.M.the Queen on her visit to Sark in 1957. Katharine and Prince Philip are just behind them.

On his retirement, he was appointed Governor of Guernsey where he received a visit from the newly crowned Queen and the Duke of Edinburgh. He was always rather proud of his bushy "Elmhirst" eyebrows, which were status symbols in the R.A.F. As a child I remember my amazement when he rolled up his shirtsleeve to show me a spectacular coloured snake tattooed up his arm. At a later date I remember him beginning to tell me about one of Ataturk's legendary parties, but Aunt Katharine came into the room and said, "That's enough, Tommy!", so I never heard the end of the story.

When he died his full title was Air Marshal Sir Thomas Elmhirst, KBC, CB, AFC. Full details of his 22 medals and decorations and his appointments can be found in his entry in Who's Who. A less formal, but entertaining account of some of the more colourful moments in Tommy's life (which included setting up a brothel in Cairo) can be found in a book called "Recollections" which was published privately by his son Roger in 1991 and printed by Whitstable Litho Printers Ltd.

He was survived by his daughter Jane (Mackie) and son Roger though, sadly, Roger died in 1999. After the death of his wife Katharine in 1965, Tommy married Marian Ferguson. He died on the 10th Nov 1982.

JAMES VICTOR ELMHIRST

Born at the Vicarage, Laxton, on the 17th October 1898, Vic was educated by governesses before being sent to prep school at Stancliffe Hall and then to Marlborough.

On leaving school in 1917, Vic enlisted and was sent for officer training at R.M.C. Sandhurst (A Company). He later transferred to the R.F.C.[1] and got his wings in 1918, but, with the end of the war, no more pilots were needed so he was ordered back to his Regiment and sent out to Mesopotamia with the York and Lancasters (or the Cork and Doncasters as they were sometimes called with humour in recognition of their main recruiting areas).

Vic Elmhirst at Marlborough.

Vic, according to brother Richie, failed to hit it off with his Colonel. He thought it had to do with an inspection by a General whose particular interest was latrines. Vic had seen to it that every bucket was spotless, but had been unable to resist the temptation of placing a rosebud in the bottom of each bucket. The General was not amused. Perhaps as a result of that, Vic was sent with a small unit, mounted on camels, to patrol a desolate area of Mesopotamia between Baghdad and Tehran with instructions, "to find out what the damned Bolsheviks are up to."

Another legendary incident involving Vic is touched upon in Leonard's F.B. letter of 16th July 1918. As I heard it, Vic was travelling to Nottingham in uniform but, as he was expecting to be met by a low ranking driver, his dress was verging on the casual. Unfortunately for Vic, as he stepped

---

1 Royal Flying Corps.

from the train in his carpet slippers, he was met by a red-tabbed staff officer and his aide. That led to serious trouble: "Sackbut, dulcimer and all kinds of music," according to Leonard.

Vic as a young subaltern.

After several years, with Leonard's help, Vic bought himself out of the Army. Shortly before he left he wrote to his parents: "I'm still agog with Leonard's cable and have told the C.O. I shall probably submit my papers within 2 or 3 weeks." He then followed Leonard to study Agriculture at Cornell for one year. On his return he was invited to help at Dartington, which had just been established by Leonard and Dorothy. In the early years of 1925/26, when Leonard and Dorothy were often away, Vic took on the role of Estate Steward.

In 1925 the school at Dartington was being set up. By 1928 Vic and John Wales had been appointed joint heads on a temporary basis while the search was on for a permanent head. Vic continued as general administrator and adviser to the trust until 1939 when it became apparent that more financial control would be needed. Heads had to roll and one of them was Vic's. Perhaps Vic's sympathies lay more with the managed than with the managers, as when he and Sean O'Casey (the Irish playwright) sent a letter to the Dartington News lamenting the axing of the Travelling Repertory Theatre by the Dartington Trustees. In spite of that, Vic's association with Dartington continued as manager of the school farm, but he moved away from the estate to Aish House at Stoke Gabriel where he farmed and grew apples. He also maintained his contact with the school through the summer camp and the sailing club. He died on the 18th February 1958. He was survived by his wife Helen and his children, Judith Ann (Webber) and Christopher MacGregor Elmhirst.

Leonard and Vic at Dartington.

RICHARD ELMHIRST

Born 6th May 1900 at the Vicarage, Laxton, like his brothers, Richard was educated by governesses before being sent to prep school at Stancliffe Hall and from there to Rugby. In old age Richard recalled the problem of the Elmhirst governesses. By one estimate they had totalled twenty-eight, but this was not the fault of the children. Papa would choose a young attractive governess with whom Mama would soon find fault. It was then Mama's turn to choose an older, less attractive, governess as a replacement. In a few months Papa would find fault with the newcomer so he could make the next choice. And so it went on.

Richie at Rugby in 1916.

Richard also remembered log splitting as a family activity. This was Papa's scheme to have his boys split logs for fencing stakes. For some reason the older boys were paid at the rate of 2/6d for fifty stakes whereas the three youngest boys only got 1d for six stakes, which led to improved arithmetic and protests from the young ones.

Richie as a young man.

After leaving school in 1918, with a cup for winning the Public Schools sniping competition, Richard reported to the Barnsley Recruiting Office on the 6th Sept 1918 and was sent, for training in the Household Brigade Officers Cadet Battalion at Bushey. He wrote to brother Pom to describe a memorable Battalion concert got up by fellow cadet George du Maurier, who brought six stars from the London stage including the composer of the musical "Chu Chin Chow". He passed his training and in March 1919 he was gazetted 2nd Lieutenant, Coldstream Guards.

That lasted until November 1919 when Richard dined with Leonard and Capt Frank Salter, the Dean of Magdalene College, Cambridge, who said: "Why not come to Magdalene?". Despite his lack of qualifications, Richard, with Leonard's help and a College bursary, entered Magdalene College after demob to read agriculture. After two years at Cambridge, he failed his exams. He was then articled to Bernard Wilson, the Land Agent managing the Frickley estate of Mrs Warde-Aldham at Hooton Pagnell, near Doncaster. After two years there, Bernard took Richard on as a partner upon payment of £250.

A year later Richard opened an office in York where he lodged with his brother Pom at 7 Tower Place on the Ouse. There he was recruited to play cricket for the Yorkshire Gentlemen with Pom and their cousin, Jack. He even signed up as a signalman for 10 days during the General Strike, during which time he managed to de-rail a goods train at Poppleton junction, York. Then in 1925, following this meandering start to working life, Richard was invited to Dartington by Leonard where he was made an employee. After a short poultry course at Cornell University, Richard returned to run the Dartington poultry department, although he also made time to skipper the Dartington Cricket Team.

In 1929 Richard married Louise Soelberg, an American dancer based at Dartington. Their daughter Eloise was, to a large extent, brought up in the nursery of her cousins Ruth and William at Dartington Hall. Richard resigned from Dartington in 1936. He wrote later that, although he was wrapped up in the delights of Dartington, he had lost all interest in running a profitable poultry department. By then Louise was employed by Ballet Jooss and, presumably, estranged from Richard who headed for America, ending up in the Chicago of Al Capone. With some financial help from Leonard and a part time job working for the International House at Chicago University, Richard studied Social Philosophy with the intention of becoming a personnel officer.

In March 1939 Richard began divorce proceedings against Louise, citing Basil Langton (the actor and director) as co-respondent. However, in spite of amiable relations between the parties, the divorce became much more complicated and expensive when, in December 1939, Richard applied for American citizenship without telling his English lawyers. The divorce eventually went through in May 1940. Louise wrote to Pom at this time: "I will write to your father and he (Richard) can tell your mother, or not, as he thinks best." Richard, knowing his mother to be a devout Christian, presumably kept quiet.

In 1942 Richard joined the American Air Corps as a private, but after only eight days of basic training he was pulled out to become an instructor. Perhaps his former existence as a second lieutenant in the Coldstream Guards had been discovered. By July 1944 he was a lieutenant and had received a citation for achievement at Iwo Jima in the Pacific. Back in Britain, Richard's future wife Morna was engaged in a search for a farm where they and Morna's young sons, Piers and Mark Haggard, could live on Richard's return from the Far East.

Richie in the U.S. Air Corps.

Richard married Morna in February 1945 and went for the first time to see Muckhart Mill in Clackmannanshire which Morna had already bought. At first they farmed, but later the land was rented off and the old mill was converted to a hotel for unaccompanied children. The hotel, or hostel perhaps, was really run by Morna who had phenomenal energy and presence. Richard played the farmer for those children who had no idea what a farm was. One of his jobs would be to take a couple of the uninitiated children (often from Hampstead or Knightsbridge) in search of Maudie the free range cow who would be milked into a pail on the roadside verge where she happened to pause in her search for the best grass and flowers.

Richard died on the 6th March 1978, just over a year after Morna's death and two months before their son Alan, who was tragically crushed to

Richie relaxing in his favourite moccasins.

death by a tractor at Muckhart Mill. Richard's daughter Frances married and moved to Australia. She has since died. His daughter Eloise and her stepbrothers Piers and Mark Haggard, now live in England. Alice (Sudaya), his daughter by Morna, lives in Australia.

Richard and Pom at Houndhill.

ALFRED OCTAVIUS ELMHIRST

Born on the 25th July 1901 at the Vicarage, Laxton, like his brothers he was educated at home by governesses before being sent to prep school at Stancliffe Hall and then to Winchester College. He was always "Pom"[1] to close friends and family.

His first memory at three years old was of being twisted up in the swing at Laxton by his brothers Vic and Richie. On falling off as the swing unwound he recalled yelling more than necessary in the hope that his mother would come out and tell his tormentors off, which she did. Perhaps an early manifestation of his political skills! Later on, in 1912, he remembered watching a solid tyred open charabanc driving down Sheffield Road into Barnsley carrying the victorious Barnsley team and Harry Tufnell, the scorer of the winning goal, holding aloft the F.A Cup.

Pom in 1912 with spaniel. (Tony)

At Winchester his scholastic achievements were modest, but in shooting and cricket he showed more talent. He was a member of the Winchester shooting VIII (as marker) in the year that it won the Public Schools Ashburton Shield at Bisley. He failed to get into the school cricket second team after a spat with Douglas Jardine (the future England captain) who wrote him off for not attending nets when he was shooting for the school, but Pom's revenge came when he led his house cricket team to victory for the House Shield, even though his house had none of the best cricketers in it.

---

[1] As a very small child, his nightly prayer was: "God bless Mummy, God bless Daddy and make me a good little boy." For some reason he could only end with, "Make me a good little Pom." This delighted his older brothers and the name stuck.

Pom with the victorious Winchester shooting XIII after their success at Bisley in 1919.

Pom's House (Finley's) at Winchester with his housemaster, A.E.Bloomfield, holding the House Cricket Cup. Summer 1919. Pom is seated on the far right.

His housemaster's joy at the victory can be explained by the Machiavellian tactics employed by the housemaster in order to have Pom as house captain. To be captain one had to be a prefect, but to be a prefect one had to be in first remove (lower sixth form), which Pom was not, because he had not reached the appropriate academic standard. His housemaster overcame this problem by moving Pom into first remove anyway. As Pom entered his new maths class, the collaborating teacher said: "We will be doing calculus this term, Elmhirst. You won't understand a word so please bring a good book and sit at the back." No league tables in those days!

Upon leaving school, there was to be no idling at University for Pom. As the war had ended, he was immediately articled to his Uncle Charles (perhaps as a replacement for Willie). His resolve to become a solicitor was put to the test on failing his final exams for the second time when the Atcherley twins (or possibly one of the Leadhams), his friends in York, invited him to join them in selling motor cars to the well-to-do of York and lent him a Bugatti Straight Eight for a few days by way of encouragement. Plan B was to emigrate to Australia with a young woman whose father owned a large farm there.

Pom and Conus on his belt driven 3 ½ HP Triumph (given to him by Auntie Min on his becoming an articled clerk).

None of that impressed his Uncle Charles who pushed his nose back to the grind stone. He managed to pass, on his third attempt, the last Law Society exam to test a candidate's knowledge of medieval copyhold land tenure. However, life in the office at Lendal was not all drudgery. With his cousin, Jack, another cricketing fanatic, he was able to practise late cuts and leg breaks in the clerk's room with a ruler and a ping-pong ball, and a waste paper basket for a wicket. When the delicate matter of a telephone was raised in the early 1920s, Uncle Charles was not prepared to have such a new fangled device in his office, but his nephews were able to persuade him on the grounds that it would only be used to enable them to raise better teams for the Yorkshire Gents C.C. However, it is not clear how Uncle Charles was persuaded to allow a typewriter to be introduced into the office around the same time.

Once qualified and having had some brief legal experience in London with McKenna's, Pom was recruited by his brother Leonard to become a trustee of the Dartington Hall Trust, a role which, I believe, gave him great pleasure and satisfaction for over 50 years, as well as extending his horizons from the pit hills (or muck stacks) and sooty sandstone of Worsbrough to the glamorous internationalism of Dartington.

Roger Morel (a member of the Estate Management Committee) with Pom and Vic at Dartington in the 1950's.

In those early days Papa Elmhirst was having difficulty in dealing with the several small tenant farms which comprised the Worsbrough estate. Farms were badly affected by the depression in the 1920s and farmers were leaving the land. In 1925, Pom, with Leonard and Dorothy's financial help, approached his father and asked to be given a free hand to modernise the estate and its buildings. Papa gave reluctant consent to these revolutionary ideas, saying: "I don't reckon to take my boots off until I go to bed." In 1932 Pom, on behalf of Leonard, negotiated the re-purchase of the farmhouse at Houndhill (where I was brought up) and a hundred acres or so from Captain Wentworth. It had passed out of the family by marriage some 250 years previously, having been built by Roger Elmhirst in the late 16th Century. In 1950 Leonard gave Houndhill and the estate, which he had inherited on his fathers death, to Pom (the sitting tenant).

Pom at Round Green (around 1980).

From then on, the farm and Pom's interest in local politics eclipsed his legal practice, although he continued to put in a twice weekly appearance at the Sherburn-in-Elmet office for the next 50 years (stubbornly withstanding an annual retirement dinner for the last ten of those years). On his death, at the age of 94, he was the oldest solicitor in England still to hold a practising certificate.

Locally he was seen as a man of apparent contradictions: a old style squire, but also a stalwart member of the local Labour party from the late 1930s and on hobnobbing terms with Arthur Scargill who still lives in one of the former farm cottages at the bottom of Houndhill. Pom was considered stubborn by his father who was appalled when, in 1936, Pom announced that he was going to marry a farmer's daughter some 15 years younger than he was and not from the same drawer at all. Such was his concern that Papa asked Leonard if he would offer Pom £100 not to marry Gwen Binder, which Leonard refused to do. Papa Elmhirst did not dare approach Pom direct, writing to Leonard: "He always was obstinate, he will be even more determined to go ahead with his imbecilic scheme if I ask him not to." In spite of that shaky start, Mum fussed over her new in-laws with such care and devotion that she soon became their favourite daughter-in-law.

Pom lived to 94. By the end his mind would drift a bit, but always in character and often residing in his favourite period, the English Civil War. A few months before he died, I found him one evening sitting in his chair by the fire. He expressed concern about The Petition of Right (1628). "I'm worried that it's not going to get through Parliament," he told me. I said I thought it was certain to get through. "I have it on good authority," I added. "That's a relief," he said.

He died on the 3rd April 1995, leaving his wife, Gwen, and children, Richard Nicholas, Paul Binder (me), Elizabeth Sarah and Timothy Genn. Characteristically, he left his body for medical research, but his memorial service at St Mary's Church, Worsbrough, was packed out.

IRENE RACHEL ELMHIRST (BARKER)

Born on the 4th September 1902 at the Vicarage, Laxton, Irene Rachel was the first and only daughter after a run of eight sons. She was educated by governesses until she was deemed old enough to be sent away to boarding school. She attended The Manor House School at Brackley, followed by a short spell at Heathlands in Malvern Wells, a domestic science college where she learned more French, book keeping and music, as well as how to run a household. She was usually referred to in the family as "Irene Rachel"(with "Irene" in three syllables).

At home she took part in most of the male activities, including shooting and rat catching. An evocative old photograph shows her on a raft on the pit pond at Pindar Oaks with two of her brothers, Richie and Vic, in the water below. On one memorable occasion she became stuck up a tree she had been climbing with her brothers. One of the boys ran in to the house to tell his devout mother, "Irene is stuck up a tree and can't get down." "Then I shall pray for her," said Mama without moving from her chair. Irene survived that drama, presumably with God's assistance.

Irene Rachel (left) with her Brackley friend "Wicked" Stubbs.

One of her F.B. letters (2nd June 1918) reveals some remarkable cricketing ability when the opposing girls school cricket team was bowled out for no runs in two overs. As Irene was the only girl who could bowl over-arm, one has to assume that she must have had a direct hand in the massacre (although every ball would have to have been straight which is no mean feat in itself). By her last year at school Irene Rachel had got the measure of her headmistress, the unpredictable "Old Fearsome", and was made head girl. However, as a letter to brother Richie makes clear, this honour had not diminished her spirit. "I think," she wrote, "I must have found Old Fearsome's weak spot because she is awfully nice to me except when I do something very wicked, but then you have to do something at school or else it would be dull." (Readers may note that her school friend on the attached photo is "Wicked" Stubbs!)

A youthful Irene Rachel in a hat.

In 1924, when Irene Rachel was a good looking 22 year old, she was invited by her brother Tommy to join him for the season in Malta where he was commanding a flight of flying boats. The Mediterranean fleet was in and the Queen of Rumania was guest of honour at Admiralty House. Following a visit by the Queen to view Tommy's flying boats, the Queen's hostess, Lady Brock, invited Irene to join the Queen for tea. This honour created mayhem in the social chicken coop on the island as a squadron of society ladies should have received such an invitation in preference to Irene Rachel, who carried it off and returned to England in triumph. A letter from Richie to Leonard illustrates the changing attitudes of the time. He wrote:

"Mother thought Irene ought not to go to a dance without a chaperone. Chorus all round, 'Oh mother, chaperones are quite out of date.'"

In 1931 she was rewarded for her work with boys' clubs by being made an M.B.E. In 1933 Irene Rachel was asked to act as hostess to His Royal Highness Edward Prince of Wales on his visit to Barnsley to open the newly completed Town Hall. The reason for the invitation, according to family tradition, was that the Prince was not prepared to sit throughout the

Irene Rachel gardening.

Irene Rachel standing next to the Mayor at the opening of Barnsley Town Hall in 1933. On the other side of the Mayor is H.R.H. Edward, Prince of Wales.

celebratory dinner with a boring Alderman on each side, so he demanded a pretty woman, and got one. A photo of that event (and Irene Rachel) still hangs in the Town Hall. At the time she was still doing voluntary work for boys' clubs in the district.

She married George Barker in 1935. He was a huntsman of some note, having been appointed joint master (with Lord Allendale) of the Badsworth Hunt. Sadly, after being demobbed from the army, he was killed in a fall from his horse in 1945 while out hunting, leaving Irene Rachel a widow with two daughters. Irene Rachel remained at Badsworth Kennels near Pontefract until 1947 when she moved to Scarlett's Farm at Twyford, near Reading. As well as being a keen gardener, she made time to become a County Councillor. She kept in close touch with her brothers throughout her life, especially Leonard and Tommy. She died on the 6th September 1978 at Scarlett's Farm. She was survived by her daughters, Anne (Fisher) and Tisha (Lady Monson)

This shows the district to the south west of Barnsley containing the following dwellings and farmsteads referred to in the letters:

Pindar Oaks: which the family rented when they moved to Barnsley 3 years after the death of William Elmhirst (Father of William Heaton Elmhirst) in 1899. (eventually it became the maternity home where I was born)

"Elmhirst": to which the family moved on the death of William Heaton's mother in 1916.

Ouslethwaite Hall: owned by the family.

Houndhill: purchased by L.K. Elmhirst from Capt Wentworth in 1933. (Having been out of the family's ownership for 230 years)

Round Green: occupied by Auntie Min, the sister of William Heaton Elmhirst.

Coumes.: a small tenanted hill farm retained mainly for its shooting.

Bitholmes: a small tenanted hill farm retained mainly for its shooting.

Foldrings: a small tenanted hill farm retained mainly for its shooting.

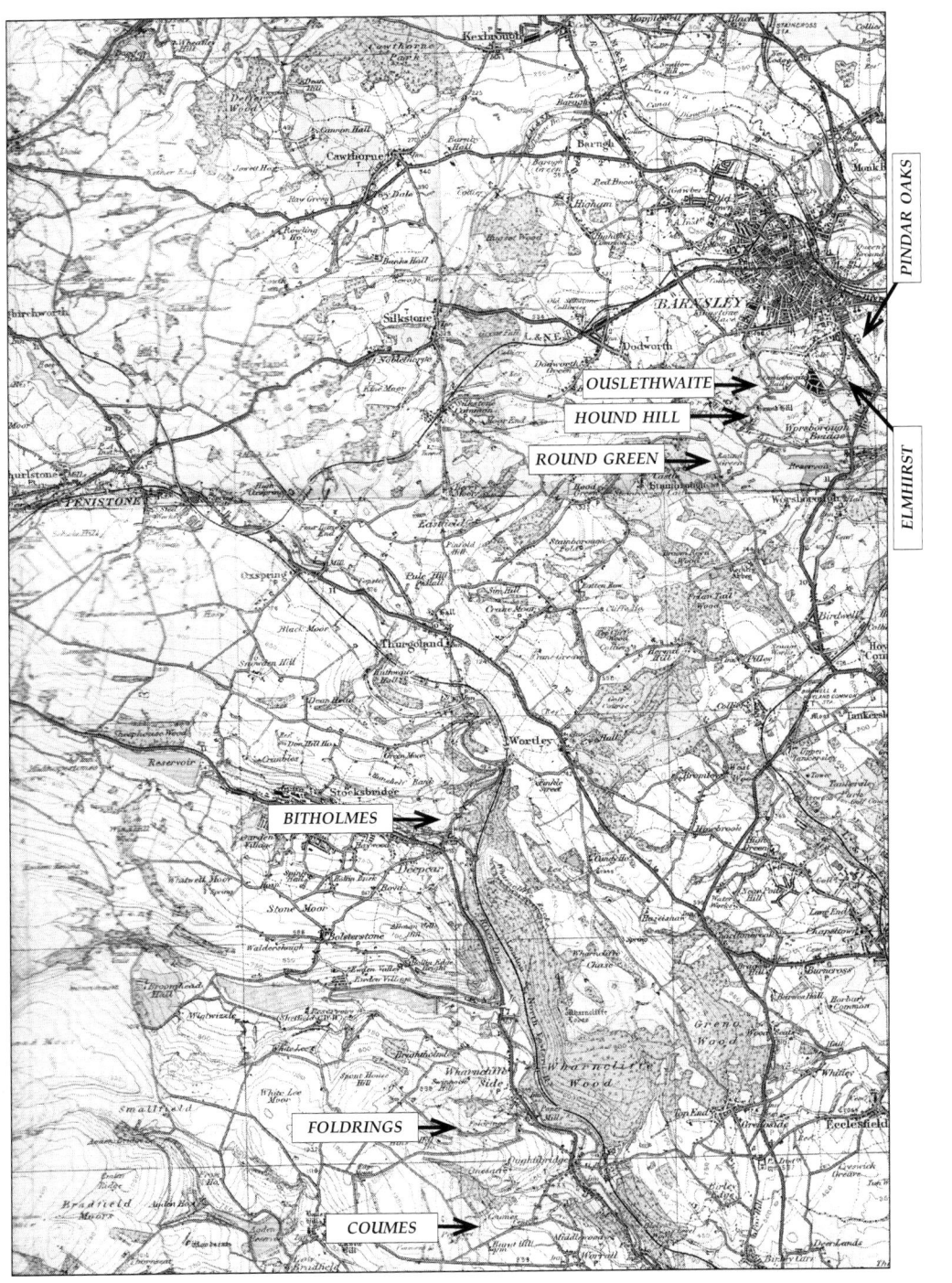

Map of Barnsley and district

BIBLIOGRAPHY

Joseph Wilkinson	History of Worsbrough	Farrington & Co London 1872
Edward Elmhirst	The Peculiar Inheritance	Privately published by E. Elmhirst 1951
Victor Bonham-Carter	Dartington Hall	Phoenix House London 1958
Michael Young	The Elmhirsts of Dartington	Routledge & Kegan Paul. London 1958
Willie Elmhirst	A Freshman's diary 1911–1912	Basil Blackwell Oxford 1969
Air Marshal Sir Thomas Elmhirst	Recollections 1895–1982	Privately published by R. T. Elmhirst 1991

Elmhirst Family Tree

WILLIAM ELMHIRST
b. 1.1.1827 d. 16.4.1899
m. ANNE PASMORE

Children of William Elmhirst and Anne Pasmore:

FANNY ELMHIRST (AUNTIE FAN)
b. 16.7.1855
d. 4.2.1940

WILLIAM HEATON ELMHIRST
b. 23.11.1856
d. 8.9.1948
m. MARY KNIGHT

CHARLES ERNEST ELMHIRST (UNCLE CHAS E) SOLICITOR
b. 12.7.1858
d. 24.6.1940

MARY ELIZABETH ELMHIRST (AUNTIE MIN)
b. 12.1.1860
d. 30.5.1944
m. THOMAS MANN
(PARENTS OF COUSINS MARJORIE, AND NAN WHO MARRIED C.S.W. HAWKESWORTH)

HERBERT JOHN ELMHIRST (UNCLE BERTIE)
b. 16.6.1861
d. 19.5.1930
m. M.E. BUTT
(PARENTS OF COUSINS JACK AND CECIL)

EDITH ELMHIRST
b. 1864
d. 30.5.1950

Children of William Heaton Elmhirst and Mary Knight:

LEONARD KNIGHT ELMHIRST
b. 6.6.1893
d. 16.4.1974
m(1) DOROTHY W. STRAIGHT
(2) SUSANNA ISAACS

ERNEST CHRISTOPHER ELMHIRST
b. 25.12.1894
k/a 12.8.1915

THOMAS WALKER ELMHIRST
b. 25.12.1895
d. 10.11.1982
m(1) KATHARINE BLACK
(2) MARIAN FERGUSON

EDWARD ELMHIRST
b. 1897
d. 1898

JAMES VICTOR ELMHIRST
b. 17.10.1898
d. 18.2.1958
m. HELEN M. MacGREGOR

RICHARD ELMHIRST
b. 6.5.1900
d. 6.3.1978
m(1) A. LOUISE SOELBERG
(2) MORNA HAGGARD

ALFRED OCTAVIUS ELMHIRST (POM)
b. 25.7.1901
d. 3.4.1995
m. GWENDOLINE BINDER

IRENE RACHEL ELMHIRST
b. 6.9.1902
d. 7.9.1978
m. GEORGE BARKER

Next generation:

WILLIAM ELMHIRST
b. 9.1.1892
k/a 13.11.1916

RUTH WHITNEY ELMHIRST (1)
m. MAURICE ASH

WILLIAM KNIGHT ELMHIRST (1)
m. (1) HEATHER WILLIAMS
(2) VERA STRACHAN
(3) HEATHER ?

CAROLINE JANE ELMHIRST
m. MICHAEL F. MACKIE

ROGER THOMAS ELMHIRST
m. CELIA R. JACQUES

JUDITH ANN ELMHIRST
m. JOHN WEBBER

CHRISTOPHER MacGREGOR ELMHIRST

ELOISE ELMHIRST (1)
m. CECIL O (JOHNNY) SHARMAN

FRANCES M. ELMHIRST (2)
m. CHRISTOPHER WILLIAMS

ALAN R. ELMHIRST (2)
m. MARION ?

ALICE C. ELMHIRST (2)

RICHARD N ELMHIRST
m. JENNIFER M.E. CROSLAND

PAUL B. ELMHIRST
m. PHILIPPA A HARVERSON

ELIZABETH S. ELMHIRST

TIMOTHY G. ELMHIRST
m. JULIE BAKER

ANNE BARKER

PATRICIA BARKER
m. NOEL FISHER

m. JEREMY MONSON